SOME
KIND *of*
GENIUS

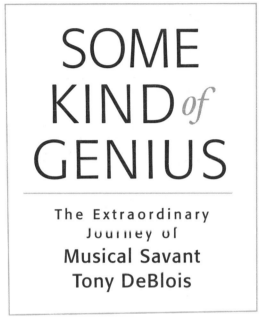

SOME
KIND *of*
GENIUS

The Extraordinary
Journey of
**Musical Savant
Tony DeBlois**

Janice DeBlois *and* **Antonia Felix**

RODALE

Rodale Inc. makes every effort to use acid-free ∞, recycled paper ♻.

Book design by Christina Gaugler

Library of Congress Cataloging-in-Publication Data

DeBlois, Janice.
    Some kind of genius : the extraordinary journey of musical savant Tony DeBlois / Janice DeBlois and Antonia Felix.
        p.   cm.
    Includes bibliographical references.
    ISBN-13 978-1-59486-273-1 hardcover
    ISBN-10 1-59486-273-7 hardcover
    1. DeBlois, Tony. 2. Musicians—Biography. 3. Savant syndrome—Case studies. 4. Savants (Savant syndrome)—Case studies.
I. Felix, Antonia. II. Title.
ML419.D455S66 2005
780'.92—dc22
                                     2005017139

Distributed to the trade by Holtzbrinck Publishers

2   4   6   8   10   9   7   5   3   1   hardcover

We inspire and enable people to improve their lives and the world around them

For more of our products visit **rodalestore.com** or call 800-848-4735

To my parents, who taught me a good work ethic; to my sons, Tony and Ray, who are my heroes; to Bo and Bill Winiker, who have been Tony's mentors; to all the teachers, attorneys, advocates, and musicians who have been a part of Tony's journey; and to those who have taken the time to listen to the heart of a young man who is beyond words.

—J. D.

Music is your own experience, your thoughts,
your wisdom. . . . They teach you there's a boundary
line to music. But man, there's no boundary line to art.

—*Charlie Parker*

CONTENTS

ACKNOWLEDGMENTS

THIS BOOK WOULD NOT HAVE BEEN possible without the generous input of many people in Tony's life, to whom the authors are deeply grateful. Thanks go to Marianne Bieber, one of his earliest piano teachers; Tom Sogaard of the Pierre School District; Adele Trytko and Storm Barkus, teachers at the Perkins School for the Blind; Paul Barringer, Tony's first jazz ensemble director and piano teacher at the Music School at Rivers; Suzanna Siftcr, an amazing jazz artist and teacher from the Berklee College of Music; and Gregory Badolato, Rob Rose, and Bob Mulvey, three Berklee educators whose devotion to music education is making the world a better place.

Thanks also go to Marc Cabot, to Jim and Kathy Nelson of the Timber Lake and Area Historical Society for their insights and direction, and to James E. Fahey of the Watson Museum and Research Center in Braintree, Massachusetts, for his knowledge and guidance.

Special thanks go to Bill and Bo Winiker, whose professionalism and warm friendship continue to shape

Tony's life. Ted and Alex Kurland helped to make the book a reality. The authors are also grateful to Tony's brother, Ray, and to Tony's girlfriend, Cydnie Breazeale-Davis, for their contributions to telling Tony's story.

And finally, deep gratitude also goes to Darold A. Treffert, MD, one of the world's leading experts on savant syndrome who so graciously gave of his time to talk about Tony and the mysteries of this phenomenon.

PRELUDE

BORN THREE MONTHS PREMATURE, musician Tony DeBlois weighed less than two pounds when he came into this world; and as a result of the oxygen therapy that kept him alive during those first harrowing months, he soon became blind. Suspecting early on that Tony had developmental problems, Tony's mother, Janice, came to learn that he was autistic, too. But some autistics have exceptional abilities—savants, they're called—and in Tony's case, his particular genius clearly was in music.

The first hints of Tony's talent came when he was two years old. Janice was searching for an interactive toy that would motivate him to sit up without help. One day, while browsing at a garage sale, she found what she believed was the perfect item: a toy chord organ. When Janice got home, she removed the organ's legs so that Tony could reach the keys comfortably while sitting on the floor. She placed the organ in front of Tony, led his hands to it, and waited for his response. Tony immediately began slapping the keys and, to Janice's delight, he sat up for as long as she would let him play.

The organ quickly became Tony's favorite toy. At age three he shocked his mother by not only playing back, note for note, songs he heard on the radio, but also playing *harmony* to songs he heard on *The Lawrence Welk Show* on TV. At five, Tony drew his first crowd—to a music store in El Paso—when he began playing "Dueling Banjos" from the movie *Deliverance* at lightning speed on a grand piano while the owner of the store chimed in from across the room to make it a duet. People who heard the music through the open door came in to see who was playing and were amazed to find a blind, five-year-old boy performing so skillfully. At the end of the piece, the crowd erupted in loud applause. That day, Janice learned that the store offered organ lessons, and soon afterward she signed Tony up. These lessons were the first steps toward Tony's very real career in music, a career developed against all the odds.

Tony's story takes us on a journey into the world of the *prodigious savant*, the rarest form of savant syndrome. According to the leading expert on savants, Darold A. Treffert, MD, the child who displays an ability that is spectacular in light of his or her disability is a *talented savant*, while the much rarer child, a *prodigious savant*, exhibits an ability that would be considered extraordinary even for a normal person. Dr. Treffert, who was interviewed for this book, recognized Tony as a prodigious savant when he first studied documents and videos about Tony in 1989, and he subsequently met Tony to do an interview for NBC's *Today Show*.

What sort of wiring occurs in the brain that allows a child to play perfectly a complex melody and harmony on the keyboard after just one hearing, yet does not give him the ability to tie his own shoes? What condition graces a teenager with an uncanny talent for playing sophisticated, intricate jazz improvisations, yet does not give him enough intelligence to make change or tell time? Tony's story offers the world a fascinating glimpse into this realm, which continues to baffle science. As Dr. Treffert points out, Kanner's classic early infantile autism is a rare condition occurring in about five to seven cases out of ten thousand children, according to current estimates. Within that group, prodigious savants such as Tony are even rarer. According to Dr. Treffert's book *Extraordinary People: Understanding Savant Syndrome*, fewer than one hundred cases have been reported in all world literature on the topic during the past one hundred years.

While Tony's story sheds light on one of psychology's most mysterious areas, it will also, the authors hope, inspire parents of autistic children to learn that there are no limits to the human mind or spirit. As Tony's music teachers are keen to note whenever they talk about him, without his mainstream immersion into music programs, Tony might still be the same withdrawn, nearly mute individual he was when he was first diagnosed as autistic at age five. But anyone who meets Tony today encounters a vibrant, curious, happy young man who loves to play the piano as well as dozens of other instruments and who can carry on a conversation as if he had been talking since age two instead of age fifteen. Tony's current schedule of performances throughout the world proves that the diagnosis of infantile autism was correct, but the prognosis and outcome were all up to Tony, his mother, and the music.

Chapter One

PRAIRIE ROOTS
and WONDER SHOWS

I am the family face;
Flesh perishes, I live on,
Projecting trait and trace
Through time to times anon.

—*Thomas Hardy, "Heredity"*

ON A SPRING DAY IN 1989, a small group gathered in Performance Room 3E of the Berklee College of Music in Boston for an unusual audition. A fifteen-year-old pianist named Tony DeBlois had made a big impression on a Berklee adjudicating committee during a recent high school jazz festival. The judges had not met Tony personally, but they had heard him play as a member of the Rivers School of Music jazz ensemble at the festival. During that performance, the stage was set up in such a way that Tony's back was to the judges; all they knew was that he played with a well-developed jazz vocabulary and outstanding musicianship.

Based on that performance, Tony was awarded a Certificate of Musicianship and a five-hundred-dollar scholarship to Berklee's five-week summer high school performance program, which gave young musicians a chance to work with some of the world's best artists and teachers. Tony had been awarded a Certificate of Musicianship at the previous year's festival, too, but the scholarship was an exciting new opportunity. In a letter from Berklee admissions director Steve Lipman, Janice DeBlois learned that the scholarship was slated for sixteen-year-old students in the last year of high school. Janice called Lipman to ask him what Berklee could do to help Tony utilize the scholarship in spite of his age and other considerations. Tony, she explained, was blind and autistic, and they would need to discuss how to help him participate in the summer program. Lipman arranged an audition, at which time key members of Berklee could hear Tony play and observe what kind of impact his disabilities might have in the classroom.

Janice arrived with Tony at the audition and took him directly to the piano. The members of the committee stood around the piano, anxious to hear him play. Gathered for this audition with Lipman were Rob Rose, director of Berklee's special programs; Dave Weigert, chairman of the piano department; Paul Schmeling, of the piano faculty; Bob Doezema, guitarist/composer and assistant director of the summer program; and famed saxophonist-turned-educator John LaPorta, one of the legends of the school.

They had all sat in this space countless times before, listening to hopeful young musicians from all over the world. Berklee, the planet's top college of contemporary music since its founding in 1945, boasts an alumni list that is a veritable who's who of jazz, rock, electronic music, and other genres, and students know that getting accepted means they'll get the best training available in their field. Berklee alumni include composer/producer Quincy Jones, saxophonist Branford Marsalis, film composer Alan Silvestri, guitarist Al Di Meola, modern big band leader/composer Toshiko Akiyoshi, pianist Diana Krall, saxophonist Bill Evans, singer-songwriter Melissa Etheridge, members of Aerosmith, and many others.

Tony started the audition with a short classical sonatina, then moved on to one of his favorites, George Gershwin's "I Got Rhythm," complete with his improvised insertion of the *Flintstones* theme, which revealed his clever and original approach to the piece. Those brief moments were a revelation. The committee realized that they had a formidable talent on their hands, a rare, special boy whose playing contrasted sharply with the rest of his behavior. When the committee members asked Tony and Janice to sit with them for a chat, they observed that some of his unusual traits could pose a problem at the school. Tony was restless for a teenager; he rocked back and forth in his chair, seemed unaware of the conversation going on around him, and interrupted the conversation with outbursts of "Let's play, let's play." He appeared to be in his own world, and no one in the group had ever met a young man like him before. Tony's blindness would prevent him from taking traditional sight-reading classes, and it also raised questions in the committee's mind about how he could learn music (did he read Braille music?) and study music theory.

"He was a little hard to control, he couldn't stay focused, and he would just blurt out things," said Rob Rose. "It was obvious that he had skill on the piano, but it was also obvious that he was going to be disruptive in the classroom. There was a lot of potential there in terms of the music, but what do you do with it, we wondered?"

Even though Rose and the rest of the Berklee committee had no idea how Tony would do with the other students or how he would act in a classroom situation, they were unanimously convinced that he deserved a chance to use his scholarship. Rose immediately called special meetings to build a program and handpick the best teachers for Tony. From the start, Berklee president Lee Berk (after whom the school was named) was personally involved in helping Tony get the most out of the program. John LaPorta, who had been so moved by Tony at the audition that he went to his studio to write a piece for him, an instrumental called "Tony's Song," was selected as one of Tony's teachers. In the coming months and years, LaPorta would become one of the most important mentors in Tony's life. Rose also selected Suzanna Sifter, a brand-new piano teacher at Berklee who was finishing her master's degree at the New England Conservatory, as one of Tony's instructors.

Tony was scheduled to take ear training, theory, keyboard labs, instrumental labs, and private lessons, just like the other students. An assistant was assigned to help Tony get to his classes and to tape-record his classroom sessions so Tony could work on the material at home with his mother.

In the first few days, Tony still had the outbursts, rocking, and inattentiveness that he had displayed at the audition. But Rose and the teachers stuck by Tony patiently, eager to see if mainstreaming him into the regular student group would have an effect. "People were sort of figuring the whole autism thing out back then," said Rose. "Even the experts weren't that expert at that time. We all thought . . . if we mainstream him, we're going to find out a whole lot of information." Putting Tony in the program was an experiment on everyone's part, and no one could predict how he would deal with the new setting, new people, and new musical challenges.

Tony surprised everyone. The difference in his piano performance at the end of the five-week session was dramatic. His interactions with outstanding young musicians in the jazz ensembles brought his playing up to a new level, revealing his ability to match the skills of those around him. Tony's technique, such as his hand position and his posture at the piano, also improved significantly. He showed his theory teacher that he understood major concepts from his theory class, such as the difference between the blues, which is a 12-measure, I-IV-V chord progression style, and a standard song, which is a 32-bar form with another particular chord structure. Like his classmates, Tony could identify the style of a piece and tell his teacher what it was.

Janice, Rob Rose, and everyone involved were thrilled with Tony's musical development, but they were even more excited about another set of changes. In just over a month, Tony had transformed from an asocial and barely speaking child to one who listened, comprehended, and responded to others. He had memorized the sounds of everyone's voice—and their footsteps—so that when someone entered the room and asked, "Hey,

Tony, how are you?" he would stop what he was doing and ask, "Hi, Rob, how are you?" Rather than randomly bursting out with a word or two, Tony now listened, reacted, and put complete sentences together. "We were most happy that he was now able to function more as a person; that was the thing that was sort of shocking to everybody," said Rose. "Nobody knew what to expect because all the information we had from the experts said that this kind of thing doesn't happen."

Janice had never dreamed that Tony could improve his communication skills so dramatically in such a short time. Like the teachers and administrators at Berklee, she was willing to give Tony a chance at being mainstreamed, but, also like them, she had no idea that it would have such a speedy, profound effect. Suddenly, Tony was more *here*, more awake, more in the world. It was a miracle, and it was just the beginning.

❦ Because Tony was born and raised prior to most of the research that has now been done on autism, Janice was on her own in many ways, using keen observation and a mother's intuition to improvise methods that would help her son develop. Her dedication, perseverance, and downright stubbornness at times were essential to getting all the rights and resources he needed. These traits would become even more important after her second surviving son was born with his own developmental problems and special needs. Meeting the day-to-day challenges of raising these two boys required the ability—and willingness—to always give more than 100 percent. Fortunately, Janice came from a long line of people with just these qualities. An overview of this family heritage reveals much about the roll-up-your-sleeves attitude that has served Janice so well in bringing up her own family.

Weaving back through several generations, Tony's roots led back to the Old West. On his mother's side, Tony's story begins in Dakota Territory, where homesteaders fulfilled their dreams of staking claim to their own piece of the prairie. Tony's great-grandmother, Daisy Mildred Beechey Stepanek, was conceived in Dakota Territory; and by the time she was born in the summer of 1890, the Territory had given way to the new states of North and South Dakota. Daisy grew up on a farm near Aberdeen in the northeast corner of South Dakota, where the land spreads flat in all directions and farmers can watch the weather move in slowly from the west.

Daisy's father had homesteaded in Conde, just southeast of Aberdeen. When she grew up and married William Stepanek, Daisy moved west to the other side of the Missouri River and became a homesteader herself. The Stepaneks took over a piece of land near Timber

Lake in the hilly, north central part of the state, on the border area where the Standing Rock and Cheyenne River Sioux Reservations meet.

Farming in the Dakotas in the early part of the twentieth century was a risky, tough business, and homesteading was the most difficult way to get started. Those who succeeded were not afraid of hard work, of starting from scratch, and of finding a way to get something done that had never been done before. As Tony's story will reveal, his mother inherited these qualities in abundance. Growing up on a South Dakota farm, Janice not only heard stories about the hard lives of her ancestors but also worked hard on the land herself. The pioneer spirit was not just a schoolbook anecdote but part of her flesh and blood—a part that she would call upon time and again as the mother of a child whose needs fell through almost all the cracks of the public school system.

In order to legally claim their land, Tony's greatgrandparents had to build their own house and farm buildings, dig their own well, and improve the settlement as a successful farm for a period of five years. The Timber Lake region didn't exactly fit Walt Whitman's vision of the American prairie as "a new garden of creation," but farming was good when the weather cooperated, the dust storms cleared, and the mile-high mountains of clouds dropped rain.

In spite of its name, wood was scarce at Timber Lake. The entire Timber Lake basin area—the two-mile-long lake was just north of town—was drier than the eastern part of the state, and it even contained a series of rocky buttes that looked more like the Southwest than the prairie. Trees, like lakes, were rare throughout the state, so the four or five trees that graced the shores of the lake gave it its name. The land in the basin was too sandy for building the sod homes that were traditional in many other parts of the prairie, but by the time the Stepaneks settled in Timber Lake, the new extension of the Milwaukee Railroad was passing through, bringing timber as well as all sorts of food and other supplies. Like many other families, the Stepaneks bought timber and built a small wood-frame house and outbuildings, and they probably hard-packed the outside walls of the house with dirt in winter to provide some insulation from the subzero-degree cold.

The Stepaneks met all of their obligations for the homestead and received their patent in 1918. William's two brothers, Frank and Edward, also homesteaded nearby and received their patents in 1917 and 1920. As landowners, they had made firm roots in the new land, following in the steps of their parents, John and Mary Stepanek, who forged a new life in Iowa after immigrating from Plzn (Pilsen), Bohemia, in 1864. William, Frank, and Edward all lived on the "Six Mile Strip," the swath of land through which the ranchers herded their cattle to be boarded on the Milwaukee Railroad. From Timber Lake and other depots on the strip, the cattle were brought to two nearby towns on the Missouri River, the largest cattle shipping points in the United States at the time. Each of the Stepanek homesteads were also in view of Dog Buttes, the landmark outcroppings named after a well-known local Native American legend. According to the legend, the buttes were the home of wild animals that were part dog, part wolf. When a lost boy wandered into their territory one day, one of the dog-wolves raised him with her pups in a cave. He grew up healthy and strong with his animal family and was eventually reunited with his people. It was a legend that sat well with pioneer types, reminding them that it's possible to survive under even the most difficult conditions.

Tony's grandfather, Raymond Stepanek, was William and Daisy's only child. He married a South Dakota farm girl from Ipswich, Edna Fern Allbee, whose ancestry takes Tony's family tree in an altogether different direction.

The Allbee branch centered around an ambitious easterner who made his mark in rural Massachusetts several generations ago. Benjamin Allbee, whose name in various records sometimes appeared as Albee or Alby, left England in 1637 to escape the religious turmoil that would eventually lead to the eruption of civil war in

England in 1642. In Massachusetts, Benjamin quickly became a prominent figure in the Braintree area just south of Boston, serving in two town governments as a selectman (the local term for councilman) in both Braintree and Mendon. He is commemorated as one of the founders of Mendon on the monument that stands in the city park.

A major landowner in the area, Benjamin spent his entire life in community-building, both politically and physically. At various times and places, he was a town official, surveyor, road builder, and carpenter. In 1664, he made a historic deal with the Quinshipaug Plantation of Mendon in which he was given permission to build and run a corn mill. Powered by water flowing over the dam he constructed, the mill was the only one in the region and was described in one annal as "the first work of civilization in Milford territory." Another history described Benjamin as "a very enterprising man, a public land surveyor, and much employed in the laying out of ways, lots and common lands in early times."

After raising a large family and building several homes, Benjamin was forced to uproot his life again, this time as an old man. In June 1675, tensions that had been building in the Native American tribes of New England broke out in violence with a raid on the town of Swansea. Among other events that precipitated the violence, the

Native Americans had grown dependent upon the colonists' goods; as a result, they were forced to sell off more and more of their land to pay for them. The raids were organized by Metacom, chief of the Wampanoag, whom the colonists called King Philip. On July 14, 1675, a raiding party attacked Mendon, and Benjamin Allbee fled his home with his family. The raiders burned down his house and his mill, and Benjamin never returned to the town that he had helped found. The battles, which came to be known as King Philip's War, lasted for a year, until all the Native American forces were defeated and Metacom was captured and killed.

In his historic lifetime, Benjamin Allbee was not only central to the formation and development of one small corner of the colonies, but he was also a witness to the end of Native American tribal life in southern New England. As we shall see in a later chapter, one of his descendants—Tony DeBlois—would move with his mother and brother to the same area of Massachusetts where Benjamin had made his mark, at the time unaware that they had returned to the turf of one of their formidable ancestors.

✦ Tony's grandmother met her husband during harvest season in Ipswich, South Dakota. Edna Fern Allbee was one of twelve children born to Henry and Hazel Allbee, descendants of Benjamin who had moved west from New England. When farmers spent entire days bringing in the crops, women from surrounding farms would make meals and bring them out to the men in the fields. Edna singled out young Raymond during one of those harvest meals. As Raymond worked away on a broken combine motor, Edna sat nearby and, as Raymond recalls it, pestered him. A couple of months later, they met up again in town at a carnival and became a serious couple after that. Edna had quit high school to help out on the farm, and as a farm wife, she would run a tight ship.

Raymond was in Aberdeen because his parents, William and Daisy, had moved there from Timber Lake in 1926. To make the move, Daisy had packed seven year-old Raymond and a few possessions into their 1925 Ford and drove to the new place, while William rode on the train with their cattle, furniture, and other belongings.

Raymond and Edna Stepanek were cut from different molds, as daughter Janice recalled:

Janice's Journal | *My mother's always been in charge of our family; she wore the pants. Dad was quiet. He worked a lot, trying to do the farm and work in town. Mom even went out and helped out in the field; if something needed to be done, she was out driving the tractor. Whatever needed to be done, someone had to do it. Once we kids were old enough, we did it, too.*

The Stepaneks raised a large family on their 160-acre farm outside Aberdeen. Janice, born in 1946, had an older brother, Garry; two younger brothers, Dennis and Keith; and a younger sister, Linda. Even though Garry was the oldest, his heart condition prevented him from doing as many chores as Janice. They both milked six cows each before going to school every morning, and Janice built up her strength carrying hundred-pound bales of hay into the barn from a young age. The farmland included fields of wheat, corn, and oats as well as a large vegetable garden; and the pastures held cattle, sheep, pigs, and chickens. Janice made all the school lunches for her brothers and sister, and she also helped her mom make dinner with her first cookbook, *Cooking with Miss Gail*. The family sold chickens, eggs, and butter in town, and Janice's dad also worked in town at Farm Power Manufacturing.

Janice went to school out in the country at the Prairie View School, the same one-room schoolhouse that her dad had attended after moving over from Timber Lake as a boy. Janice's teacher, Mrs. Smith, taught kindergarten through grade 12, as had all the schoolteachers before her. Many of South Dakota's rural schoolhouses stayed in operation well into the postwar years; Prairie View held classes until 1964.

Only fourteen children attended the Prairie View School when Janice was growing up, and she and her friend Martha were the only girls. Although Martha was two years younger, the girls had a lot in common, especially in the amount of responsibility they had to take on at home. When Janice was in third grade, her brother Garry was ill with rheumatic fever, and that same year, Martha's older brother died. Both girls had to work hard at home from that point, and they were both tomboys who loved hayrides, roller-skating, and swimming in the James River. Martha also taught Janice sign language, which she had learned in order to communicate with her deaf cousin. The two girls used sign language to talk to each other without their brothers knowing what they were saying.

Janice was a good student who earned A's. The only problem she ever had with her teacher was the day she was given her first phonics book and completed all the exercises that very day, much to the exasperation of Mrs. Smith, who had planned to use the book through the rest of the school year.

A field trip with the Prairie View class left a strong impression that would resonate many years later in Janice's life. The students visited a state institution, and during the trip Janice met a little girl who was playing alone with her dolls. When Janice tried to play with her, the nurses told her she couldn't, and she had to walk away. Later, Janice learned that the children at the home were mentally retarded and had been separated from their families for that reason. At that young age, she felt that it was wrong for a child to be committed to an institution because of a disability—one that she had not even perceived in the girl as an innocent child herself.

Every year, Janice moved back a row at school when the new six-year-olds took over the front row. But she never made it to the last, oldest row; when she was about to enter the seventh grade, the Stepaneks moved to Columbia so that Garry could attend high school there. His parents knew it would be easier for him to get to and from school if they lived in town. Aberdeen Junior High was an enormous change for Janice, with a different classroom for each subject and dozens of students her age. When she reached the tenth grade, the family moved again, this time to Pierre, the state capital, where her father had landed a job as an electrician in the statehouse.

The transition to Pierre High School was easier than the one from Prairie View to Aberdeen because Janice had already spent three years becoming acclimated to town life and a big school. She joined the debate team at Pierre, and she researched a topic that she would draw upon many years later when working with various school districts to obtain opportunities for Tony.

Janice's Journal

The topic of debate when I was on the team—which was the only extracurricular activity I did in high school—now seems so strange. Do you know what we debated? Federal Aid to Education. I was on the side that was arguing against the aid. Later, I would benefit from knowing all about those arguments, about where the federal government was coming from.

Raymond Stepanek's new job at the statehouse was the result of years of experience and skills learned on his own through a home study course in electrical engineering, which earned him a certificate to work in the trade. Raymond had always been obsessed with electronics, from the ham radio he built with part of his crop money to the patent for an air compression system he designed. Among the projects he worked on for the state was building the microwave paths for the South Dakota Highway Patrol communication system. Raymond's children grew up watching their father constantly tinker with electronics at home, and Garry and Janice both became familiar with all types of wires and circuitry. Janice hoped to work in electronics one day like her father.

≪ During Janice's earliest years living out on the farm, the boys she knew at the Prairie View School had always seemed like brothers. But at Aberdeen, Pierre, and other places Janice visited, all the young men were new—not only the students, but those young men whom she met in other, unexpected ways. In the summer of her sophomore year, for example, Janice took care of her cousins in Tilford while her aunt Penny was in the hospital having another baby. Tilford, in the Black Hills on the western border of the state, had a population of twenty-eight, and everyone knew what everyone else was doing. The whole town knew that Freddie Goff was dating Janice, the girl who would soon go back home to Pierre. When Freddie came to visit Janice and her family two years later at Christmas, Janice's brother Garry hooked up a microphone to the radio and broke into the program, saying: "We interrupt this broadcast to ask, 'When is Freddie going to pop the question?' " Freddie did ask Janice to marry him that day, and he gave her a ring. Janice thought they would get married after she graduated, but, oddly, she never heard from Freddie again.

Janice worked the night shift at the restaurant in the new Holiday Inn during her senior year at Pierre High

School. This was the first "nicer" restaurant in Pierre, and it was always busy with people associated with construction of the Oahe Dam on the Missouri River seven miles north of town. The Army Corps of Engineers project, begun in 1948, would finish during Janice's senior year in 1963. President Kennedy had officially dedicated the dam the previous summer, and when finished, it would provide electrical power to North and South Dakota, Montana, Nebraska, and Minnesota.

Janice took a cab to and from the restaurant every night, and she often got the same driver. Louie was always interesting and charming, but he was curiously unpredictable in his moods. Sometimes he was wildly outgoing, even putting on a Southern accent and telling tales about Nashville, and at other times he was quiet and more interested in listening to Janice. After six weeks of dating, Louie asked Janice to marry him, and they agreed to elope. It was hasty, and Janice didn't tell her parents because she and Louie didn't have anywhere to live, and Janice wanted to stay at home until she graduated. Their elopement wasn't secret for long. During the three-day waiting period for their marriage license, the application notice was published in the newspaper, and Janice's mother got a call from a friend congratulating her on the marriage. Edna blew up and demanded that Janice leave the house. The couple rented an apartment from Louie's father, and Janice began a journey down a road that was destined to be rocky from the start.

First, Janice learned that she had literally married the wrong man. Louie's brother, Leslie, also drove a cab; and even though he wasn't a twin, he looked very much like Louie, down to the haircut. The quiet, more introspective side of Louie that Janice had been attracted to wasn't Louie at all, but his brother, Leslie. When Janice saw Louie and Leslie together for the first time, she was shocked, then humiliated, that she could make such a mistake. But it was too late. Not only was she married, she was pregnant. She also believed that marriage was forever, and she didn't know of anyone except Hollywood starlets who ever got divorced.

"I was numb when I realized my mistake," Janice recalled. "I kept saying to myself, 'You stupid thing, you!' There was so much going on at the same time. We got married in April, and within just a couple of weeks my father-in-law was in the hospital after a horrible accident. I was pregnant, so there wasn't time to think about mistakes. Right away I was dealing with morning sickness. I was so young that it was almost overwhelming."

After Leslie became Janice's brother-in-law, he and Janice did not discuss the mix-up or any feelings they still had for each other. "People didn't discuss things like that back then," Janice said. But on Leslie's wedding day a few years later, the family had gathered at Leslie's house before the wedding. As they were all about to leave for the church, Janice and Leslie went into the bedroom to gather everyone's coats and purses. "Our eyes met," said Janice, "and I could see he was as sorry as I was about what had happened. It just never worked out for us, and we never discussed it."

While taking her final exams in English class, just before graduation, Janice began breaking out in red spots. She went to the school nurse, who recognized the outbreak as rubella, German measles. The nurse had to ask Janice if she was pregnant, because the disease would have a devastating effect on a fetus. Janice, who could be as stubborn as her mother, told the nurse that it wasn't any of her business. As a result, the nurse didn't warn Janice that a woman infected with rubella in early pregnancy had a 20 percent chance of having a baby with birth defects.

The spring of 1964 was full of crises in Janice's life. She had been thrown out of the house, she was sick and pregnant, she had a husband who often didn't come home till late, and her new father-in-law had just been severely burned in an oil tanker explosion at the railroad

yard where he worked. The stress was alleviated somewhat when Janice's parents invited her to move back
home, with Louie, in a small apartment they set up in
their house. The prospect of a grandchild softened their
disappointment in Janice's marriage, and they rallied
around her.

Janice and Louie's daughter, Sonja, was born in
February 1965; and from the beginning, the baby
showed signs of serious health problems. By the six-
week checkup, Sonja's head had grown abnormally
large. The doctors diagnosed her with hydrocephalus,
an increase of cerebrospinal fluid around the brain. In
addition, an examination at eight months revealed that
she was deaf. The doctors and social workers recommended that Sonja be put into an institution, and they
drew up all the papers. Janice, recalling the lonely little
girl and the other children at the state home she had
visited in her Prairie View days, couldn't bear the
thought of Sonja being in one of those places. Sonja's
prognosis was very poor, and spending her last weeks in
a state institution seemed merciless. The night before
the papers were to be signed, Janice was called to the
hospital. The baby, at nine months old, had taken a
sudden turn for the worse. By the time Janice arrived,
Sonja was dead.

Sonja Louise was constantly in the hospital—if she was

home for two weeks, she'd be back in the hospital for a week. It was all so sad and unexpected. I was brought up in a time where all we learned in health education class was that you got married, you had kids, and you lived happily ever after. I imagined that being married was going to be like the TV shows Father Knows Best *and* Leave It to Beaver. *Having a very sick baby was never in that picture.*

The night before Sonja passed away, I dreamed that she died. In the dream, we buried her in a little white casket with gold handles on it, and she was wearing a yellow sweater set. The next day, after she actually died, we went to Thompson's Funeral Home in Pierre to pick out the casket. She was two inches too long for the one we originally selected, and we ended up choosing a white casket just like the one I saw in my dream. I had a cute pink sweater set I wanted to bury her in, but there was a formula stain on it, so we went downtown to get a new sweater set with a hood to cover the little stitches on her head. We couldn't find a pink set, so we had to get a yellow one, just like in my dream. I had had nine months to prepare for this, but it was still so hard to let her go.

❧ In the midst of everything, Janice was pregnant again; however, soon after Sonja's death, she had a miscarriage. Louie announced that he was leaving for several months to work on a combine crew that traveled from Texas back up to South Dakota, and he told Janice that she could stay with her parents. "I didn't get married to live with my parents," she told him, and she announced that she was leaving, too. The carnival was in town, and the owner had offered her a job. "You want to go to Texas, fine; I'm joining the carnival," she said. Janice took "Smitty" up on his offer to join Smith Wonder Shows, which was headed north.

Janice's stint with the carnival wasn't long, but she spent enough time on the road with the Wonder Shows to get a firsthand glimpse into carnie life. Her job was on the midway running the cork gallery, where shooters lined up to try to knock down small cork figures. The carnival workers stayed in cheap motels and were always on the move; they formed a close-knit group. Unaware of the unwritten rules of carnie social behavior, Janice made the mistake of walking around the grounds one night with another carnie, only to turn him down when he wanted to go steady. Janice soon learned that their walk meant that she was supposed to "be his," but she wanted nothing to do with him. With one carnie complaining of wounded pride and a couple of other men in the carnival headed toward a fight over her, Smitty kicked Janice out of the show before things got worse. Smitty's job was to maintain order in the carnie family; he couldn't tolerate any infighting, so the new girl was out.

Suitcase in hand, Janice moved back to Aberdeen to work at the restaurant at the Champlain Truck Stop, which was managed by her uncle Don. He and Gertrude Young (the mother of Janice's school friend, Martha) also managed the restaurant at the bowling alley in Aberdeen, and they needed the help. Although she was able to room with Martha, who had an apartment in Aberdeen, Janice wasn't happy back in her childhood town, and she decided to move back to Pierre. On her first day in town, Janice took a job as a cook in a small café, and she went out that night to celebrate. As fate would have it, she ran into Louie, and, still vulnerable to his charms, she reunited with him for a time. She didn't leave him behind for good until February 1967, when their divorce was finalized.

✦ At twenty-one, Janice was free to do whatever she wished. One career option, she figured, would provide on-the-job training as well as food, clothing, and shelter. There was a military recruitment station in Pierre, and one day in March 1967, Janice walked into the office and applied to each branch of the service. Prepared to enlist with whomever accepted her first, she ended up signing with the army. Janice enlisted in the Women's Army Corps, and she was scheduled to take basic training at WAC headquarters in Fort McClellan, Alabama.

Janice's army recruiter at Fort Pierre told her that with training as a communications center crypto specialist, she could eventually obtain a radio license with a radar endorsement, the highest license possible in the electronics area of the military. That licensure would qualify Janice for good jobs once she got out of the army. She knew that radio operators were always sent to Vietnam, but she was willing to go if that's what it took to get a license.

To Janice's surprise and great disappointment, though, when she finished basic training and transferred to Fort Gordon, Georgia, she learned that the army didn't train women for the radio license because only those trainees headed for combat in Vietnam were considered. Women were not sent into combat, and the WAC units that were set up in army headquarters at Long Binh and in General Westmoreland's headquarters in Saigon did not require women radio operators. Janice could train as a communications center crypto specialist, but this would not lead to a radio license.

Studying codes and secret communications analysis in the cryptology program was still interesting and much more challenging than any of the jobs Janice had held back in South Dakota. She knew she was working toward something, even though it wasn't the path she had originally set out to take.

Army life was all about routine, but now and then something happened to stir things up. Janice had left the Smith Wonder Shows the previous year, but a member of the show had remained smitten with her all that time, dreaming up his own version of their future. One day, in Fort McClellan, Janice got a message that she had a visitor. One of her carnie buddies was standing in the office, all smiles. He announced that he had followed her to Alabama, had bought a house, and was ready to make a life with her. To add to the shock, he proposed to her on the spot. Janice felt bad that he had gone to so much trouble, but she turned him down anyway. His visit was completely out of the blue, and she never found out what became of him after that.

Other than the offhand surprise visits and glitches in her initial career plans, army life wasn't bad. Janice was transferred to Fort Hood, which lies about halfway between Dallas and Austin in central Texas. There, she enrolled in Vietnamese classes out of her personal interest in studying languages. At Fort Gordon, she had taken a course in Iranian, and she thought Vietnamese would be another interesting challenge. Janice had another motive as well: If the rules changed and she were permitted to take the radio course, there was a chance that she might still be sent to Vietnam, where her language studies would be a benefit.

While Janice worked as a communications specialist at Fort Hood, some of the worst events of the war were raging overseas. On January 31, 1968, the North Vietnamese launched the Tet Offensive, a simultaneous attack on hundreds of cities and towns, including a raid on the seemingly impenetrable US Embassy in downtown Saigon. This was the great turning point that galvanized public opinion even more powerfully against the war. Television brought the aftermath of the gruesome embassy attack into fifty million American living rooms, and the scope of the attack forced the majority of Americans to acknowledge that the war was unwinnable. By March, approximately six thousand American and South Vietnamese troops had been killed in the Tet Offensive, as well as fifty thousand North Vietnamese. Public support for the war plummeted even further after the My Lai massacre of March 16, when American soldiers killed one hundred peasants, including women and children, in the village of My Lai.

In 1968, the military suffered the highest casualties of the war with 16,589 troops killed—an average of more than 1,300 each month. By January 1969, the US deployment in Vietnam reached its peak of 542,000 troops, and it remained at about 500,000 for the last five years of the war.

Stateside, antiwar protests heated up following the Tet Offensive. Students at Columbia University in New York staged their famous occupation of the administration building in April 1968, and protesters clashed with police at the Democratic National Convention in Chicago in August. Meanwhile, at Fort Hood, as in every other base in the country, troops, officers, and staff went on with their business. Janice worked on her Vietnamese grammar and vocabulary in her spare hours, and she began spending more time with her favorite Vietnamese instructor, a tall, blue-eyed, bright young Spec 5 from Utica, New York. Owen Mooney had served in Vietnam as an interpreter with the 501st Military Intelligence Battalion; but after a jeep accident, the doctors discovered that he had thyroid cancer, and he was shipped home. Owen had surgery to remove his entire thyroid gland and followed up with radiation therapy.

Owen was easygoing yet full of energy and, at age twenty-one, "the youngest E6 (staff sergeant) in the history of the US Army," according to Janice. They both joked that they were sent by military intelligence to spy on each other. Owen headed up a group of fellow soldiers who found time to make up an elaborate role-playing

game in which they created an army of their own—
enlisted men were officers; officers were enlisted men—
and played it to the extent that they typed up fake orders
for each other. Owen also used the surgery scar across his
throat as fodder for war stories with his buddies.

Owen and Janice became serious enough to talk
about getting married and having a family. But their
hopes about children were quashed when Janice learned
from Owen's army dog tags that his blood was Rh positive. She was Rh negative, and the combination of the
two in a pregnancy could produce an Rh-positive baby.
In that case, the mother could produce antibodies that
would attack the baby's bloodstream and cause brain
damage and possibly death.

The news was devastating for Janice, but she and
Owen still wanted to go ahead with the marriage. They
resolved themselves to the fact that they wouldn't be able
to have a family, and they looked forward to making each
other happy.

They flew up to Pierre to get married, and that week
Janice took Owen to her doctor so he could run the
required blood tests for the marriage license and also
explain in detail why their blood types prevented them
from having children. The doctor looked at the test
results and saw that Owen was Rh negative. The information on his dog tags was wrong, so the couple learned

that they could have a family after all. "We realized that Owen had gone through Vietnam with the wrong blood type in his chart," said Janice. "They just got it wrong. So we were ecstatic."

Owen and Janice were married on September 6, 1969, and soon after, Janice considered leaving the army. Her request went through the system, and she was officially off-orders in November with an honorable discharge, as army policy allowed at the time. Not long after they were married, Owen got orders to spend a year studying Korean at the Defense Language Institute in Monterey, California. Army rules allowed Janice to join him and also take Korean classes herself.

The language school was founded by the army in November 1941 to teach Japanese to Japanese-American soldiers so they would be prepared in the event of a conflict with Japan. War broke out after the attack on Pearl Harbor a month later, so the school continued and eventually moved down to the Presidio (Fort) of Monterey, on the Monterey Peninsula about ninety miles south of San Francisco. Spending a year at the Presidio of Monterey was like a luxury vacation in some ways, as it is located in one of the most spectacularly beautiful spots in the country. Tourists flock to Monterey County for the beaches, rocky cliffs, Big Sur coastline, and quaint seaside towns such as Pebble Beach, Carmel, and Monterey.

For Janice, the beautiful surroundings, the classes, and her happy marriage were shadowed by the personal sadness of a series of miscarriages. After having four miscarriages in the first three years of the marriage, she was pregnant again. Classes ended, and Owen got new orders to go to Korea. Janice moved back to Pierre, closer to her family, to wait out his assignment.

In 1971, Janice was finally carrying a baby to full term, hoping that at last everything would be all right. But it wasn't to be. She got the news that the baby was in danger. The army rushed Owen home on emergency leave. On October 8, Janice gave birth to a baby boy, Aaron, but he was not the healthy child she had prayed for. Aaron was born with only the brainstem section of his brain, liver abnormalities, and a club foot, and he survived for only sixty hours.

Janice and Owen didn't give up hope of having a family, however. After Owen's emergency leave from Korea to Pierre, he was allowed to stay stateside with a transfer to the Sixth Cavalry Regiment at Fort George G. Meade, Maryland. With this transfer, Owen went to work for the National Security Agency (NSA) headquartered at the base. Fort Meade lies about halfway between Baltimore and Washington, DC, and Owen and Janice rented a house about ten miles north of the NSA in Glen Burnie, Maryland.

This transfer gave Owen the opportunity to work for the cryptology agency, which employed more mathematicians than any other organization in the United States and probably the world. The agency was launched in 1952 with two missions: to design cryptology systems that would protect the United States and to analyze and find weaknesses in enemy code systems.

Everything that goes on at the NSA is top secret, of course, and Owen couldn't talk shop when he got home, even though Janice was well versed in his line of work. But Janice made her own foray into intelligence work, landing a job as a private investigator for two companies in the Baltimore/Washington, DC, area. Her first assignments were doing security for TOP department stores, then Lerner stores. Janice sat behind the window in an office high above the floor, watching customers and employees through binoculars. Suspected shoplifters, most of whom were juveniles, were tracked down, paperwork was filled out, and sometimes Janice had to go to court to present her evidence to the judge. In addition to shoplifters, Janice apprehended vandals, such as one man who came into the clothing section one day, drew a knife, and slashed an entire rack of leather coats. There were unscrupulous clerks to keep an eye on, too; one salesclerk at TOPS sold four thousand dollars' worth of merchandise to his friends over a period of a few days while ringing up only four dollars for each purchase. Part-time, Janice also worked security for Pinkerton's, Inc., as a "guardette" at Colts games in Baltimore's Memorial Stadium.

❦ The army relocated the Sixth Cavalry to Fort Bliss, Texas, in 1973, and Owen had orders to move with them. He and Janice packed up house again and set off for the state in which they had met. The contrast between Maryland and West Texas was dramatic; Fort Bliss is just outside El Paso, where Texas borders Mexico and New Mexico. El Paso is in the Chihuahuan desert, and the city gets less than nine inches of rain per year and endures about two weeks of temperatures above 100 degrees at the height of summer. The desert land that spreads out beyond the city is dotted with shrubs, prickly pear cactus, and mesquite trees—all a far cry from Maryland's deciduous trees, moderate temperatures, and forty inches of annual rainfall.

Like everything in Texas, Fort Bliss is big—larger, in fact, than the state of Rhode Island. The base covers an expanse of 1.1 million acres that extends about fifty miles north into New Mexico. In some ways, for Janice, moving to El Paso was like going home to South Dakota— wide-open spaces, a big sky, and drives out in the country for miles without seeing another car. Janice and Owen rented an attractive red brick house in a western section of El Paso called Del Norte Acres, just adjacent to Fort Bliss. Most of the people in the neighborhood were older, but they soon met another young couple, Carl and Carol McCauley, who had also just moved to El Paso and who lived one block away.

Carl was the new assistant minister at Hyland Presbyterian Church in the neighborhood, and Owen and Janice started attending his church. Janice soon decided to get baptized and make church a more regular part of her life. Carol was a role model of sorts—a minister's wife who wasn't puritanical and subservient to her husband but just a regular, independent woman.

Janice's Journal

Carol and I became good friends. She was very much a person of her own. She didn't care if her husband was a minister in the church; she had her own life, too. She and I did canning together, even brandied pears together. I had always wanted to go to church, but I wanted somebody to go with, to share my experience. Owen was fine with that. We had talked about going to church when we were first going together at Fort Hood, but we never really went to church until we moved to El Paso. I got baptized at the church in El Paso because I decided I was going to be a mom, and I needed to change my life around!

Janice realized that she was pregnant in 1973 when she got dizzy standing on some scaffolding twelve feet above the ground at her new job. She had finally found work in electronics, even though she had applied at the Burns Company in El Paso for a private investigator position. Mr. Burns didn't have any openings for investigators, but he did need an electronics technician to install alarm equipment. During her interview, Janice described all the skills she had learned from her father and on her own. Burns was convinced enough to give her a chance, and Janice became the first woman he had ever hired to install burglar alarms.

Getting a job in electronics was an unexpected, exciting turn that fit in with the fresh start Janice felt about the move to El Paso. Her days at the Burns Company were numbered, however. While wiring a system near the ceiling inside a manufacturer's warehouse one day, Janice got dizzy and nearly passed out. Some coworkers got her safely down, but when the boss heard about what happened and learned that Janice was expecting, he didn't want to take any chances.

"That ended my career installing burglar alarms," said Janice. "I was pregnant with Tony."

Chapter Two

THE GIFT

O body swayed to music, O brightening glance,
How can we know the dancer from the dance?

—W. B. Yeats, "Among School Children"

Antonia Felix: Tony, what does music feel like to you?

Tony DeBlois: I think of myself as a dancer when I'm listening to music. Marie [a friend who teaches dance] says, "Listen to the beat, one, two, three." I'm getting the hang of it now. Me and Cydnie [Tony's girlfriend] both know the dance steps. Playing music is really great. Whenever I learn a new song, it just feels really good. Just after hearing it one time.

Antonia: What's your favorite activity during the week?

Tony: Singing in the choir. In the church choir. I do bass, but I can do other parts, too. When we did the Handel's *Messiah* on Easter morning, I know how to do the tenor. I like that high part [sings]: "And he shall reign. . . . " I really got into that high part! Isn't that something?

Antonia: What are your dreams for the future?

Tony: My next goal is to meet Ellen. I like listening to Ellen DeGeneres on TV. Another challenge for me is to play with the Boston Pops. Bo's friend [Bo Winiker is Tony's trumpet teacher] is going to work to get me to play with the Boston Pops. He already took my business card. Isn't it good? Bo said, "I think you should play piano with the Pops." Also Broadway, a Broadway show. We're busy working on a play [at a local school] called *Shakespeare Comes to Calamity Creek*. I like backing the students in a play. The director says to me, "Can we take it from that section?" And I know right away. He says, "Can you play that spot again?" and I say, "Yes." I have to transpose the key because they're little kids, and they have high voices. I transpose it for the kids so they can sing lower or higher if they want. Isn't it good?

Antonia: What is your favorite everyday sound, outside of music?

Tony: My favorite sound is the commuter rail. I've got one right near my house. I love the whistle of the train going by my house really fast. I love it! My next favorite sound is crows.

✦ Autumn is hot in El Paso; the long days of ninety-degree weather hold out through mid-October, and it's not unusual to have an eighty-degree Halloween. When Janice learned that she was pregnant in the sweltering September of 1973, she knew that this pregnancy would turn out all right. She had a powerful intuitive feeling that in spite of all the problems of past pregnancies, this baby would be born alive, and it would survive.

Janice and Owen began transforming the extra bedroom in their house into a nursery, and the Women's Guild at the church gave Janice a baby shower. Soon, the nursery was outfitted with baby furniture, including a dresser filled with crib linens and infant clothes. Even though they had been disappointed over Janice's failed pregnancies in the past, Janice and Owen were excited during these preparations, and they moved ahead with a positive attitude about bringing a baby into the world.

As usual, Janice experienced some dizziness and

fainting spells when she was pregnant this time. One such episode fell just before a holiday and put a wrench into their entertaining plans. Owen's work with the intelligence unit at Fort Bliss was secret, but Janice was able to meet many of his army friends and acquaintances. For Thanksgiving 1973, she and Owen invited a group of unmarried guys from the base to the house for a traditional turkey dinner with all the trimmings. While shopping for the elaborate dinner at the Fort Bliss commissary, Janice had a fainting spell in the checkout line. The clerks called an ambulance, and Janice was rushed to the hospital; but she repeatedly tried to explain to everyone involved that it was nothing, that she always fainted when she was pregnant. The attending physician insisted on neurological tests, however, and kept Janice, who was twenty-seven years old, in the hospital through the entire weekend.

Janice's doctor ordered her to bed rest, and she spent the next several weeks watching a lot of TV and going stir-crazy with no one to talk to all day. The newspaper and evening news were filled with updates on the Watergate scandal; pressure was mounting in Congress to impeach President Nixon over his alleged participation in the break-in of the Democratic Party's National Committee offices. The president was also in the news over his orders to bomb Cambodia during the Vietnam War, which prompted Congress to pass the War Powers Act that fall. Other top stories on the news during those weeks included the streaking fad spreading throughout college campuses and a record-breaking rush by a Buffalo Bills running back named O. J. Simpson.

Janice was in bed through Christmas and into the new year, but on the evening of January 21, in her twenty-sixth week of pregnancy, she began to have labor pains. Later in the day, her water broke, and Owen rushed her to the William Beaumont Army Medical Center in El Paso. The doctors planned on giving Janice medication to stop the labor, but she developed a fever that climbed to 104 degrees, and they decided to allow the birth to proceed.

Early the next morning, the nurses put Janice on a standard birthing table and raised her feet into the stirrups. According to hospital rules, a woman in childbirth is not to be put in this position unless there is a doctor in the room; but Janice had dilated only to four centimeters, and the nurses didn't expect anything to happen soon. As everyone would learn, nothing could be assumed about Tony, and his birth was no exception.

At 7:26 a.m. on January 22, Janice's doctor, Max V. Bryant, MD, was walking down the hall toward Janice's room. As he turned and came through the door, the baby suddenly appeared, feet first, and popped out in a spontaneous breech birth. Dr. Bryant rushed to the table and caught the baby just in the knick of time. Speechless with shock, Janice simply stared at Bryant and the tiny form in his hands. Later, one of the nurses who heard about the story said to Janice, "It's lucky for you Dr. Bryant is the catcher for the baseball team!"

Anthony Owen Mooney was no bigger than a puppy at birth, weighing one pound, nine ounces. Dr. Bryant immediately began an Apgar test, the reading to check a newborn's vital signs. The Apgar score, taken at one minute, five minutes, and ten minutes after birth, evaluates heart rate (pulse), breathing rate and effort, responsiveness to stimulation, activity level (muscle tone), and appearance (skin coloration).

A perfect Apgar score adds up to 10, with two points given for each category. Tony's Apgar score was for heart rate only because he did not respond in any of the other areas, and these three readings were 1, 0, and 1. With these low numbers, as well as the breathing and other problems anticipated with such a premature infant, Dr. Bryant intubated the baby in the delivery room, connected him to a respirator, and rushed him to neonatal intensive care.

The hospital had just opened a brand-new, state-of-the-art neonatal unit, staffed by the first generation of doctors who had completed training in the new field of neonatal medicine. Without the technical advancements and special clinical training that supported this unit, a preemie like Tony, born at just six months, had little chance of survival. Tony put the staff through their paces that first day, clinically dying approximately one dozen times. His condition required repeated stints on the respirator and large doses of oxygen. One night during those first tense weeks, pediatrician Olin "Chip" Mauldin, MD, kept Tony breathing with a handheld, squeeze-bag respirator connected to a tiny face mask. Dr. Mauldin held Tony and "bagged" him with this respirator throughout the night.

Respiratory distress syndrome (RDS), common with premature babies because the lungs are the last organs to develop, forced Tony's doctors to give him oxygen and to keep his fragile air passages open with a machine that delivered continuous positive airway pressure (CPAP). The air we breathe contains 21 percent oxygen, but as Dr. Bryant wrote in the chart, "The baby was maintained on and off the respirator for a long time requiring concentrations of oxygen up to 100%. . . . On 20 Feb he was placed in Oxyhood at 50% with very slow weaning to room air and multiple episodes of respiratory arrest during this weaning for which he required resuscitation and bagging."

Tony's critical breathing problems kept him on the

brink for several weeks, but they were just one set of crises that he endured during his four-month stay in the hospital. From the start, Tony was diagnosed with possible sepsis, an infection of the blood; anemia; hyper-bilirubinemia (too much bilirubin in the blood); a heart murmur and irregular cardiac rhythm; a mouth infection called oral thrush; and several bouts of pneumonia. When he was twelve days old, a cut in the main artery of his right leg produced a blood clot that traveled to his abdomen, where it tore a hole in his colon. This went undetected until that night, when Dr. Bryant, who was putting on his coat and about to go home, returned to the nurse's station on a hunch and ordered an x-ray for Tony. The x-ray revealed that air was escaping into the abdomen from the bowel, and Dr. Bryant ordered immediate surgery for a resection and colostomy. Janice was astounded that Dr. Bryant decided at the last minute to take an x-ray; if untreated, the problem would have been fatal. "It was just a fluke," she said. "God was watching over him."

Theodore T. Katz, MD, the surgeon who performed Tony's emergency surgery, took one look at the patient on his operating table and described him as "no bigger than a rat!" The surgery went smoothly with no complications, but during his recovery, Tony became allergic to the adhesive on the bandages as well as to his own stool.

His skin was red and raw, and Janice—who had not yet held her baby—was anxious to help. She suggested crushing up milk of magnesia tablets with cornstarch to make a soothing powder that would take some of the acidity out of his stool. Because Tony couldn't withstand the adhesive that connected him to the colostomy bag, Janice also suggested replacing the bag with a "belly binder," a small cinch that mothers used to wrap around their infants to prevent their navels from protruding. Janice hunted down a set of belly binders in a dusty corner of the Ben Franklin store in El Paso, and the combination of the powder and the new wrap cleared up the problem. "It worked wonders," Janice said. "All the doctors wrote it down in their little notebooks."

In late February, Janice was finally given permission to hold her baby as well as to help with his feedings. Tony wore infant disposable diapers that were cut in half—preemie diapers hadn't been invented yet—and his first feeding spoon was a wooden coffee stirrer. The nurses gavage-fed Tony through the nasal gastric tube that all premature infants require because they aren't strong enough to suck, swallow, or breathe while feeding. Tony's feedings alternated between gavage and bottle feeding, and Janice was allowed to do every bottle feeding. In mid-March, Tony ate his first solid food, one teaspoon of rice cereal fed from a tiny med cup. Tony began to hold on to Janice's and the nurses' fingers as they held him. On his one-month birthday, Janice gave him his first toy: a soft, five-inch-tall giraffe that he could curl his tiny hand around when he wasn't being held.

Although the feedings were supplemented by a constant IV of fluids and nutrients throughout his hospital stay, Tony gained weight very slowly. He was put on soy formula when doctors discovered that he was allergic to milk, and he used so much energy fighting to breathe that he had the strength to eat only very small amounts of the formula and rice cereal.

From time to time, Janice took breaks from the hospital to get things ready for Tony to come home. She shopped for baby clothes but couldn't find anything small enough until she walked down the toy aisle at the Ben Franklin store one day. There, hanging in packages on tiny plastic hangers, were outfits for sixteen-inch dolls that appeared to be the perfect size. Janice bought red corduroy overalls, a blue-and-white gingham shirt, and some pajamas. At home, she tore out the seam of the inside legs of the overalls and sewed a tab of snaps in their place, and she also sewed a "Big Leaguer" patch on the front bib. Janice dressed Tony in the overalls and gingham shirt outfit more than in anything else those first few months, until he was big enough to get into regular newborn clothes.

While Tony was in intensive care, Janice and the nurses were convinced that he learned how to manipulate his vital signs in order to get attention. Even though Tony barely had the strength to breathe, he seemed to know that he needed as much attention as possible, and he figured out how to get it.

Janice's Journal

There were three babies in the neonatal intensive care unit: a little girl named Ruth in one incubator bed, Tony in the middle, and a boy named Jaime on the other side of him. There were only two nurses in the unit, and when they were taking care of the two babies on the outside, Tony figured out how to lower his heart rate and his respiration, which made his sensors beep and brought the nurses over to check him out. Also, when they were standing at the doorway giving reports to the doctors, he did the same thing. When they finally realized that he was deliberately doing it, they would turn around and say, "TO-NY . . ." and his little heart rate would start to go back up!

Week by week, Tony slowly put on ounce after ounce, and by late April he was near a normal birth weight and had stopped having respiratory distress episodes. As a result, he was discharged on May 1, 1974, weighing five pounds, four-and-a-half ounces. Tony had made the record books at the hospital as the youngest premature infant to survive.

⤺ All parents have a mix of fear and excitement when bringing their first baby home from the hospital; there's no manual, they've never done this before, and they have no idea what to expect. The Mooneys had those fears, too, and they were justified in the very first week. Edna Stepanek had arrived in El Paso to help care for her new grandson by the time Tony finally came home on May Day, 1974. Tony slept in a bassinet in Janice's and Owen's room, and the three of them watched and fed him in shifts so that someone was with him twenty-four hours a day. The third night, Edna rushed to Janice with Tony in her hand; he had stopped breathing and was turning blue. With a sweep of her arm, Janice cleared everything off the kitchen table, laid Tony down, and began mouth-to-mouth resuscitation. Owen called 911, and the first unit to arrive was the fire department chief's car. Although they had a portable suction unit, neither the chief nor the fireman with him knew how to use it to resuscitate a tiny infant, so Janice took over as she had learned how to suction while Tony was in the hospital.

By the time the ambulance arrived, Tony was breathing again, and his color was returning. On the way to the hospital, Tony had another spell, and he was again revived. On arrival, the doctors suctioned Tony's air passages; and over the next thirty-six hours of his hospital stay, he breathed normally. Janice and Owen were given a portable suction device to use at home in the event of another breathing crisis.

That scare was a tough start to Tony's homecoming, but Janice and Owen knew that their child was truly a survivor. They were prepared to deal with anything that might come along. As Tony continued to grow that first year, however slowly, Janice was constantly reminded of the alternative that one of the doctors had given her the day that Tony was born. It's a memory that haunts her to this day.

Janice's Journal

When Tony was born, the first time I got to see him after having delivered him, a doctor told me that Tony was probably going to be blind because of the oxygen therapy—if he made it—and he gave me a choice to let Tony live or die. After he was born alive! They told me his lungs weren't developed. It was unfathomable to me that a child was born alive, and we were supposed to make this decision. You had this whole facility built to help preemies. I told the doctor, "I'll take whatever God gives me."

When Janice took Tony in for his six-week checkup, the effects of the oxygen therapy he had received in the first three months of his life were unmistakable: His eyes were undeveloped, and he was blind. Excessive oxygen given to a newborn causes the blood vessels in the eyes to rupture, scar, and eventually disconnect from the retina altogether. This condition, called retrolental fibroplasia, is a trade-off in neonatology. While new technology can keep premature babies alive, doctors still need to administer oxygen to compensate for undeveloped lungs, which causes blindness.

The connection between extra oxygen and blindness in infants was made in 1952. Up till then, some doctors gave newborns a few squirts of oxygen, thinking that it would help them thrive. Scientists eventually discovered the delicate balance that oxygen plays in the development of an infant's blood vessels; and in this case, more oxygen was definitely too much of a good thing. Doctors stopped the practice after this discovery; but when sophisticated technologies brought new hope to premature infants, the practice was revived, with everyone fully aware of the consequences. (According to the National Eye Institute of the National Institutes of Health, newer technology to monitor the oxygen levels of infants has helped to reduce this condition, now called retinopathy of prematurity [ROP]; and new treatments can slow the abnormal growth of blood vessels in the eye. Very premature infants are still at high risk, however. Of the 28,000 babies born each year weighing two pounds or less, about 14,000 to 16,000 develop some degree of ROP. Of those, about 1,100 to 1,500 develop ROP that is severe enough to require medical treatment such as laser surgery or cryotherapy, which freezes part of the eye to stop abnormal growth of the blood vessels. In spite of these advances, about 400 to 600 infants in the United States become legally blind from ROP each year.)

During Tony's first checkup, the doctor at the army hospital in El Paso quickly put things in motion to get Tony to a hospital in San Antonio for the eye surgery. Owen, who was out on maneuvers in the field, was called in for the emergency and joined Janice and Tony on a flight to the hospital.

The surgeons worked on Tony for a few hours, after which one came out to the waiting room to deliver the bad news: The procedure didn't work. A short time later, another surgeon came out to repeat that Tony's blindness was irreversible. When the third surgeon came to Janice and Owen with the same news, he was a bit taken aback by the couple's calm reaction; he had been prepared for an emotional scene. Instead, Janice began thinking in terms of Tony's future educational needs and focused on the practical issues.

After the three-day ordeal in San Antonio, the family faced another medical crisis that began on the trip back to El Paso. Owen suddenly became ill with a fever; and by the time they got home, he felt compelled to go to the doctor. Owen was hospitalized on the base, and the rash that broke out a few days later led to the diagnosis of Rocky Mountain spotted fever. The disease can be fatal if not treated quickly enough, and Janice was warned that her husband might die. For months she had been living with the possibility that her critically ill baby might die, and suddenly her husband was gravely ill, as well.

The health authorities could not determine where he had contacted the tick that carried the disease. He may have been bitten while out in the field on maneuvers or while walking across the grass at the San Antonio hospital. It was the first case of Rocky Mountain spotted fever they had encountered at William Beaumont Army Medical Center, and they treated it successfully with antibiotics. Owen underwent a long recovery at the hospital, while Janice took care of Tony on her own at home.

❦ One of the methods Janice used to help Tony calm down or fall asleep during the first year of his life was a new record released by Japanese obstetrician Hajime Murooka. *Lullaby from the Womb* contained four long tracks of sounds recorded in the womb of an eight-months-pregnant woman, which transported the infant to the familiar, soothing sound environment of the womb. The next two tracks blended the pulse and swoosh of the womb sounds with light classical music, and side two contained six familiar classical pieces, carefully selected for their low pitch levels and calm rhythms. "Newborns are calmed by smooth pure sound and low pitch and irritated by rough noises with uneven movement," explained the liner notes. With tracks such as the Air from Bach's Suite no. 3 (often called "Air on the G String") and "The Swan" from Saint-Saëns' *Carnival of the Animals*, this record was Tony's first exposure to classical music. Janice and Owen did not listen to classical music otherwise; their record collection spanned rock 'n' roll to standards, including the Nitty Gritty Dirt Band, Janis Joplin, Frank Sinatra, and Tony Bennett.

Janice observed in Tony's first weeks at home that he had a special affinity for music. At times he would cry loud and hard for no apparent reason. After ruling out everything that could make him uncomfortable, she noticed a pattern. He cried during the pauses between the tracks of the record album she was playing; apparently he didn't want the music to stop. Janice also learned that Tony was calmed by the rhythm of the washing machine; when it paused before the rinse cycle, he began to cry. "He thought that his crying caused the next cycle on the washing machine," she said. "He loved the sound of the washing machine."

Tony had many ailments that first year, including several gastrointestinal infections that caused diarrhea and dehydration. Problems like these continued to postpone the surgery to close his colostomy. Surgery would be scheduled, only to have Tony contract something in the hospital such as an *E. coli* infection, pneumonia, or German measles. Surgery was rescheduled many times until, finally, in June 1975, nearly one and one-half years after the colon resection surgery, Tony underwent the follow-up surgery, and the colostomy opening was sutured. This was a great relief—no more infections, constant cleanings and treatments, or catheter dilations of his bowel.

At about the time of Tony's first birthday, Janice began attending El Paso Community College on the GI Bill. Owen, who was taking courses as well, was interested in anthropology; and as a new mother, Janice was eager to take child development courses. Her first class was an introduction to psychology, and the more courses she took about behavior and child development, the more she realized how much she *didn't* know. Tony seemed to be developing slowly in some ways, but she thought it might be due to the many health crises and hospitalizations he had endured throughout his first year.

Janice reasoned that now that Tony was stronger, he might catch up; but she was also concerned that he might have some cognitive problems, and she wanted to learn as much as possible about normal child development. Comparing some of Tony's developmental milestones to those of the standard child development chart reveals that he was delayed in many areas.

TABLE 2-1

Activity	Normal Standard[a]	Tony
Coos and babbles	3 months	9 months
Holds head up	3 months	10 months
Reaches for objects	3 months	11 months (taught)
Grasps objects	3 months	9 months
Turns head toward sound	3 months	11 months (taught)
Smiles responsively	3 months	9 months
Smiles spontaneously	5 months	6 months
Laughs aloud	6 months	11 months
Rolls over	7 months	12 months
Sits alone	7 months	20 months
Crawls	12 months	20 months
Walks with support	12 months	20 months
First says "Mama"	12 months	15 months
Pulls self up to stand	12 months	22 months
Walks alone	24 months	32 months

[a] National Center on Birth Defects and Developmental Disabilities (www.cdc.gov/ncbddd/autism/actearly)

As the chart reveals, Tony didn't sit up on his own until he was two years old, and he accomplished that only with the help of an aid that would ultimately shape the course of his life. In Janice's search for a toy that would draw Tony's attention and motivate him to sit up, she spotted a Magnus chord organ at a garage sale one afternoon. The instrument was about thirty inches long and supported by four short legs. To the left of the keyboard was a series of ten buttons, five with major chords and five with minor chords. Common sense told Janice that a blind child would be enthusiastic about something that made noise. She had also observed Tony's love for listening to the stereo or the radio, so she bought the organ. Janice's recent studies had taught her that you should teach at the child's level, so she applied this to the physical level, too, by removing the legs of the organ before placing it on the floor in front of Tony. The results were dramatic.

"He sat up, swatted it with his hand, then went crazy with it for the first six weeks," Janice said. "He played every combination of notes that he could figure out. After he discovered he could make sounds with both hands, he did the chords and keys together."

Not only did Tony learn to sit up so that he could play—mission accomplished—Janice couldn't tear him away from the instrument. Rather than a blanket or a favorite stuffed toy, Tony wanted to carry his keyboard with him everywhere. When Tony got a little older, Janice had to find a substitute instrument that he could carry more easily outside the house. "He wanted to take that thing everyplace," Janice said. "I eventually bought him a harmonica so I could take him to the grocery store." Janice taught Tony how to play the harmonica by sitting behind him on the floor, putting it to his mouth, and pinching his nose so that he would have to breathe through his mouth. Tony caught on quickly and spent hours experimenting with the small instrument's sounds. Whenever they left the house, Tony had to bring his harmonica along.

Tony's attraction to music was an interesting and positive sign, but from Janice's first years at El Paso Community College, where she earned associate degrees in both education and child development, she recognized many behaviors in Tony that were not in line with the norms she was learning about in class. Rather than respond to questions or requests, for example, Tony's primary language response was to repeat what he heard. "Tony, say bye-bye to Ann" would make him respond with "Say bye-bye to Ann." Although Tony was often quiet and gentle, he also had unusual outbursts that Janice couldn't control, such as yelling out and launching into four-hour tantrums. He blurted out words rather than sentences, habitually flapped his hands, poked his eyes with his fingers, walked on his toes, rocked back and forth, and smeared his feces.

The catching up that Janice hoped Tony would accomplish in his toddler years did not occur, and she struggled to understand his developmental challenges and how to manage them.

⤙ Janice's first exposure to a full explanation of autism occurred at a lecture by a visiting speaker one night in El Paso. Janice was supposed to have class that night, but the teacher said that students could attend the lecture by Ivar Lovaas, PhD, instead. A psychology professor at UCLA, Dr. Lovaas had established a groundbreaking autism research clinic in which his graduate students helped run a thirty-five-hour-per-week program for autistic children and their parents. During the lecture, Dr. Lovaas showed a film of his students working with autistic children, and Janice said to herself, "That's what my son does. That's how Tony walks and talks." At last, she recognized Tony's collection of unusual behaviors as part of a complex disability concerning social interaction and communication. Suddenly, many things fell into place.

Janice went backstage afterward and introduced herself to Dr. Lovaas, describing Tony's behavior and asking questions about how to distinguish between blind behaviors and autistic ones. Dr. Lovaas told Janice that in the thirty years he had been working with autistic children, he had never worked with a blind autistic child. In the following months, Janice talked to Dr. Lovaas several times on the phone. She would keep in touch with Dr. Lovaas over the years, and eventually she had the opportunity to attend a daylong workshop in which she worked with a graduate student on Dr. Lovaas's treatment method, called applied behavior analysis.

At the lecture, Janice observed that most of the typical behaviors outlined in Dr. Lovaas's talk and in the film were a rundown of what she experienced with Tony every day: repeating words or phrases instead of using language normally, unresponsiveness, aloofness, tantrums, rocking, extremes of physical over- and underactivity, resistance to change, and an aversion to touch and cuddling. In addition, Janice learned that a child with autism could have vastly uneven levels of motor skills, with finely tuned abilities for some activities and no functioning at all with others. This aspect of the disability, as well as an inappropriate attachment to a particular object, were evident in Tony's obsession with his chord organ.

Tony used the organ to mimic melodies he heard on the radio. The very first incident occurred when he was two and a half years old: Janice heard the theme from the film *Lawrence of Arabia* coming from the other room. She peeked her head around the corner from the kitchen to see Tony sitting at his toy chord organ, playing. It was a bizarre sight—a tiny child playing such a sophisticated melody and getting every note right.

Tony loved the radio, and Janice listened to all types of stations throughout the day. She also played Tony a series of cassettes called *The Storyteller Presents,* in which children's stories such as Snow White, Cinderella, and Pinocchio were narrated over a background of classical music described on the cover page as "Music of the Great Masters." Tony memorized the connection between each story and the classical piece that accompanied it, as Janice discovered when they were listening to a classical piece on the radio one day. As soon as the music started, Tony shouted, "Jack and the Beanstalk!" Janice checked it out by playing the tape that contained that story, and sure enough, he had recognized the exact piece of music.

When Tony was three, he shocked Janice once again by playing along to the television during *The Lawrence Welk Show.* He sat at his little organ and played back the music he heard, using his own harmonies with his left hand and playing the melody with his right. This ability gave Janice enormous confidence that Tony was taking in much more around him than he appeared to; by interacting with music, Tony revealed his awareness of the world and his ability to respond. Although Tony used music rather than language, he had a connection with life that perhaps hinted at other connections to come. It was exciting to see this unusual ability, but even more exciting for Janice was the revelation that Tony was not absorbed in another world that no one could reach. Music was obviously the key, and Janice intended to nurture it as much as possible.

For a few hours during the week when Janice and Owen were in school, Tony attended preschool programs in El Paso, including a daycare program at the YWCA and the local school district's Preschool for the Visually Impaired. Tony's first developmental evaluation was done by the school district's Outreach Early Childhood Learning Center when he was a year and a half old. Although the report noted that evaluations done before the age of two are not "highly predictive" of future development, the testing did reveal delayed development. Tony's gross motor skills, for example, were at the six-month level, well behind his chronological age of eighteen months. Tony's language skills were rated at ten to twelve months, but overall, the psychologist who wrote the report stated that Tony's "current level of progress is encouraging." The psychologist also pointed out that Janice and Owen's involvement in Tony's development had had a great influence on how much he had developed thus far. "Tony's parents have been highly active in the parent participation aspect of our program," wrote the psychologist, Robert G. Young, "and Tony's current level of achievement would not have been possible without their cooperation and high level of involvement."

This involvement included creative proaction from the start, such as finding a way to overcome Tony's dislike of being touched. Janice and Owen brought him into their bed at least once a day to cuddle and play. "We'd play with him and roll him over and tickle him so he was getting a lot of stimulation," said Janice. "We had to teach him that it was fun to be touched." Janice and Owen were happy with the results, as Tony's overly sensitive attitude gradually gave way to a more normal response whenever anyone reached out to him.

Janice also fell into a routine of talking to Tony about everything she did in hopes that the verbal stimulation would allow information to sink in. Janice took Tony to the grocery store, where she talked about the food and invited Tony to touch and smell it. "Mommy's getting the lettuce. Can you smell the lettuce?" she would say in the produce department. Even though Tony did not clearly respond, Janice was not dissuaded. Nor was she ever tempted to keep Tony at home to hide him from the world. "She went on with her life," said Ann Lemke, Janice's counselor at El Paso Community College. "She didn't make it a secret; she didn't hide it from people; she tried to give him as normal a life as she could."

Lemke, who is also blind, recalled that, over the years, Tony was always calm in his visits to the school with his mother. "You could tell he was learning something," she said. "He wasn't unruly, he wasn't extremely hyper or hard to manage, and he would follow instructions that she gave him. When you don't know what the child is thinking, their behavior is more unpredictable, but she took him out with her like any parent would."

As Janice learned more about child development and devised ways of working with Tony, she was eager to pass along what she learned to other parents. Janice held get-togethers at her house to create an informal forum for parents to talk about their children. Janice knew from experience that learning about children's behavior in textbooks is one thing, but figuring out what actually works day-to-day in the real world is another. Janice was excited about the progress Tony made with her approach to tactile and verbal stimulation, and she wanted to hear what other parents were doing, too.

When Tony was two years old, Janice regularly visited a daycare center in El Paso as part of a practicum on child development at El Paso Community College.

Although Tony was blind as well as a year younger than the youngest children allowed, Janice talked to the director about the benefits of the staff watching her work with a special-needs child. She also pointed out that the government was in the process of mandating that 10 percent of the enrollment in federally funded daycare centers must be given to special-needs children. It was a struggle, but Janice convinced the center's director that it was a win-win situation, and Tony was allowed to attend.

While Janice was still attending school and discovering what resources were available to Tony, she enrolled him in speech therapy sessions at the University of Texas–El Paso. There, at age six, Tony worked on pronunciation as well as on many issues of understanding and communicating. In his one-hour sessions, held twice a week, Tony's therapists helped him try to use expressive language, limit his self-stimulating behaviors such as hand flapping and rocking, and improve his articulation. The sessions also included learning how to identify shapes and to understand concepts about soft and hard, sweet and sour, rough and smooth, push and pull, up and down, and others. In one term-end report, the therapist described the problems Tony brought to the sessions.

Tony displayed the following unacceptable clinical behaviors: hand flapping, eye poking, stamping of his feet, echolalia [the compulsive repetition of words spoken by someone else], temper tantrums, and inappropriate singing. . . . All of the inappropriate behaviors are not only autistic-like responses but are also mannerisms characteristic of blind persons. Tony also demonstrated poor muscle control of the head and neck, which was approached by saying, "Head up."

Although the therapists described Tony's singing as "inappropriate" for the therapy sessions, they recognized that his talent should be nurtured. "Tony has great aptitude in music," they wrote, "which should be given further research and be incorporated into the therapy setting with a teaching purpose." Perhaps Tony's love of singing could be used, for example, to help him overcome his physical articulation problems, such as his inability to move his tongue to form many words. With Janice's insistence, the therapists also incorporated music as a reward system in working with Tony. Janice had read an article in a music therapy magazine that described the positive results of playing a few seconds of music on a tape recorder after the child completed an activity. Tony was not interested in the M&M's candies that the therapists had been trying to use as a reward, so Janice told them about the article she'd read and requested that they use music instead. She recorded a few songs from the radio, including Tony's favorite, "Like a Rhinestone Cowboy," and brought the tape recorder to his next speech session. Much to the therapist's surprise, Tony responded immediately. At his next evaluation, his accuracy in each of his speech areas had gone up to 90 percent. For the next ten years, Janice made sure that the music reward system was incorporated into as many of Tony's therapy and educational experiences as possible.

❦ Janice continued to study child psychology and development after finishing her two degrees at El Paso Community College by enrolling in a bachelor of science program at the University of Texas–El Paso (UTEP), where she took a triple major in elementary education, special education, and early childhood. In addition to teaching her more about Tony, the degree would qualify her to get a teaching job in case anything happened to Owen. It was a practical, well-planned strategy that would serve her well. Janice continued to research Tony's educational options as he got older, and she became convinced that he would be best served at a school for the blind. He had attended the Preschool for the Visually Impaired of El Paso's Region 19 School

District for a time, but the elementary schools did not have classes for blind students. Janice was adamant that a school for the blind would be the most beneficial for Tony. How could a regular classroom teacher be expected to deal with a child who was blind as well as autistic?

As Janice searched for schools for the blind in the Southwest, she learned that in order to have Tony's developmental challenges on record with the state, she would need a letter from a neurologist; a letter from a pediatrician or general practitioner would not be adequate. In July 1979, when Tony was five and a half years old, Janice scheduled an evaluation for him at the El Paso Neurological Institute, where he was seen by Robert D. Schneider, MD. Dr. Schneider made the following comments in his letter for the record.

Anthony seems happy and content. He tends not to be recognizant of others socially and has no conversational speech. However, there is evidence of echolalia. Memory seems to be quite good. His mental responses are certainly inconsistent. . . . On the basis of my neurological evaluation I strongly suspect that Anthony is autistic. He certainly needs to be in an educational environment which can deal with autism as well as blindness.

Janice was grateful for an official diagnosis, as this would help her take advantage of whatever opportunities the Texas Commission for the Blind could provide. The Vocational Rehabilitation Act passed by Congress in 1973 stated that people with disabilities could not be excluded from federally funded programs or activities, and Section 504 of the act specifically granted disabled people access to education, public facilities, jobs, and housing.

The diagnosis guaranteed these rights for Tony, but the law was relatively new. Janice discovered early on that she would have to remind people of the law and, at times, threaten a legal suit in order to get the services Tony needed and deserved. Immediately after the evaluation by Dr. Schneider, for example, Janice had a conflict with Tony's daycare director at the local YWCA. When Janice told the director about the doctor's evaluation, the director said that Tony could no longer attend because they were not set up to care for an autistic child. Janice asked why the label would make any difference if they had already been caring for Tony without any problems. The director did not budge until Janice asked the president of the Texas Society for Autistic Children (TSAC) to give her a call. By this time, Janice was an alternate delegate to the TSAC, as well as secretary of the El Paso Autistic Society. Janice knew many people at both the local and state levels of the organization, and she wasn't afraid to ask them for help. The TSAC president enlightened the YWCA director about the law, described Janice's right to file a suit against the YWCA on the basis of Section 504, and ultimately convinced the director that keeping Tony at the daycare center was the right thing to do.

The incident at the Y was just the first of several situations in which Janice was forced to threaten legal action in order for Tony to obtain his legal rights. Another battle occurred over public transportation in El Paso, when Janice tried to schedule two rides a week for Tony on the Handicapped Sun City Area Transit (HandiSCAT) system. The plan was for Tony's daycare teacher to put him safely on the bus, which would drive him to the university, where Janice would be waiting to take him to his speech therapy session. Not until Janice presented her arguments to the transit system, proving that Tony was disabled and that the law granted him rights to public services, was she able to set up the rides.

When Tony was six years old, Janice believed she had found the perfect school in which he could begin a regular academic life—or as regular as possible. The New Mexico School for the Blind and Visually Impaired was located just over the border, about seventeen miles away from El Paso. Established in 1903, it was a nationally recognized public school that provided classroom instruction for children to age twenty-one, as well as many outreach services. Janice was thrilled to find a school so close that would allow Tony to attend class like any other child yet receive the special curriculum and training that only a school for the blind could provide. Janice's application process was cut short, however, when she learned that the school district would not pay out-of-state tuition for a child when there was a school for the blind in Texas. Unfortunately, that school was in Austin, about 580 miles away from El Paso.

Although the superintendent of the El Paso School District supported Janice's goal of enrolling Tony in a school for the blind, he was not the only person in charge of making such decisions. The least expensive option for the local school district was to put Tony in a regular class-room and provide additional Braille training. If Janice wanted to send Tony to a special school, she would have to make her case through the Assessment, Review, and Dismissal (ARD) process, in which she would present her arguments, the school district would present its side, and if they could not come to an agreement, the case would be given to a mediation officer to decide.

At the first ARD meeting, Janice sat at a table with a representative from the Texas Commission for the Blind, and across from them sat fifteen representatives of the school district. "They were all sitting there telling me no, my child wasn't going to the school for the blind," said Janice, "and I said yes. I guess we're going to court." The mediation officer then reviewed all the arguments and decided in favor of Tony attending the school in Austin. His transportation would be drastically limited, however, with only one flight home every semester. This was a difficult proposition to accept, but knowing that it would be a short-term solution, Janice enrolled Tony at the school.

The Texas School for the Blind and Visually Impaired was even more established than the New Mexico school, having been launched in 1856 and committed to serving children with multiple disabilities. Everything about the school was outstanding—except the unfortunate distance—and in 1980, Tony was placed at the Austin school for a six-week evaluation.

The forty-five-acre campus in a quiet section of the capital city includes residence halls where children from across the state live during the school year. Janice was very impressed by the program and extremely happy that Tony's curriculum would include music therapy and private lessons in classical piano. Janice decided that even if Tony would have to live away from home for a term until she finished school, it would be worth it to get him enrolled in such an excellent program. One of the benefits of a residential program is the round-the-clock attention to skills of daily living, which would also benefit Tony.

Although Austin had a lot to offer, Janice knew that music was going to play an important role in Tony's education and his life, and she planned to move to another city after graduation. She hoped to find a metropolitan area that had a school for the blind as well as a vibrant cultural life that would give Tony a greater exposure to music, to performing opportunities, and to teachers who were experienced in teaching piano to the blind and disabled.

When Tony's evaluation at the Austin school was complete, Janice confronted a new challenge in arranging his transportation. Austin is a ten-hour drive from El Paso, and Janice contacted the school district about his transportation for getting to school for his first semester in the fall and for his trips home during school breaks. The school district was responsible for the cost of the transportation and cleared the way for Tony to fly. Janice knew he would be fine with airline personnel watching over him and someone waiting at the gate in Austin to pick him up. But the airline wasn't quite so sure.

Continental Airlines, which flies the route from El Paso to Austin, had recently made a new policy that allowed children five years old and older to fly alone if their parents or grandparents were on either end of the trip, so age was not the factor. But the airline initially refused to fly Tony on the grounds that he could not communicate his needs, and they, therefore, could not be responsible for making sure he was all right.

With the help of officials from the school district, Janice once again pulled together her resources to make her case. She called up the new superintendent of the El Paso Region 19 School District, who explained the law to the airline and let the airline know that Janice was willing to go to court to obtain Tony's travel rights. Continental had a change of heart, and Tony was cleared to go. Just in case Continental had any second thoughts on the day of the flight, Janice invited a reporter from the *El Paso Times* to be at the airport for Tony's first solo flight. The flight staff was prepared and happy to welcome Tony on board, however; and once Janice buckled him in, he was left in the care of two off-duty flight attendants.

Janice had talked to Tony at length about the upcoming flight and helped him memorize a few things to say. "What are you going to tell the stewardess if you get thirsty, Tony?" Janice asked one last time. "I'm so thirsty, please give me a Coke," Tony said softly. The flight went smoothly for everyone, and the *Times* reporter published a story about it that week under the headline "Blind Boy Braves First Solo Plane Ride."

The assessment made by the Texas School for the Blind during Tony's evaluation stated that the six-year-old boy's language comprehension and expression were at about the two-year-old level. Tony often talked quietly, "as if to himself," stated the report, and because he could imitate so well, he was able "to repeat complex language structures that held little or no meaning for him." His strong memory was evident in his ability to " 'play back' stories, songs, and complex verbal routines [that] appear to be virtually meaningless to him, however." The speech/language pathologist concluded that Tony should receive "very carefully structured language intervention," which in the best case would be done in a classroom taught by a teacher trained to work with the visually impaired and in consultation with a speech pathologist. This type of classroom experience was available at the school, but Janice would have to fight to convince the El Paso School District to pay for it.

As far as Janice was concerned, perhaps the brightest opportunity for Tony among all the advanced methods used at the school in Austin was music therapy and piano lessons. Janice had taken another step in supporting Tony's musical talent the year before, when Tony was five, by starting him on organ lessons. She had been putting money away for Tony's college fund, knowing that blindness was not a barrier to getting a college education. Once she learned that he was autistic, however, she decided to put the money to another use.

Janice's Journal

My father had gone to school with a kid who was blind, and they used to ride bikes around together. I knew that Charlie had gone to college to become an attorney. When Tony was just blind, I had been putting money away for him to go to college, but after the autism diagnosis, I knew that college wouldn't be an option. I drew out his money from the bank and took him to the music store and asked him if he wanted a piano or an organ, and he chose an organ.

Tony's trip to the Kurland-Salzman music store that day in 1979 would become one of Janice's favorite memories from his childhood. Tony sat down at a gleaming black grand piano and started playing "Dueling Banjos," the popular instrumental from the 1972 movie *Deliverance*. Mr. Salzman sat down at another piano across the room and began playing the second "banjo" part. At first, the customers could only see Mr. Salzman, and they were confused about where the sound of the second piano was coming from. Then they spotted little Tony, nearly hidden behind the huge piano, and gathered around to hear him play. As the sound traveled out into the street, people began to wander in to form a bigger crowd.

Tony got a wild burst of applause when he and Mr. Salzman finished the song—his first experience of an audience reaction. Janice then got down to business and asked Mr. Salzman if he had any organs for sale in her price range. Someone had just returned a virtually unused Kimball Swinger electronic organ, and the price was right. The Kimball was a beginner organ with two forty-four-note manuals, a one-octave row of pedals at the floor, and a built-in rhythm section. With two keyboards at his hands instead of one and new buttons that played a variety of rhythms, Tony had a richer level of sound to play with. With the Kimball, he sounded like an entire combo when he played his two favorite songs at the time, "Let It Be Me" and "Blue Spanish Eyes."

Janice also signed Tony up for organ lessons at the store, which he would take every week for five dollars an hour. It would not take long for Janice to discover that it was the best money she had ever spent.

Janice's Journal

Before I bought the toy organ, one of the objects that I used to motivate Tony to sit up when he was a baby was an overturned Folgers coffee can. He loved to tap on it with the sticks that came with his toy xylophone. When he was little, Owen and

I would have him sitting on our laps when we played cards, and we'd tap a pattern on the table, and he would tap it back. We'd make intricate patterns, fast-fast-slow, and he'd repeat them. He had a very strong sense of rhythm from that age.

As Tony grew up, I could pat out a song on his back and he could tell me what song it was. This reminded me of something I did when my brother Garry and I milked the cows when we were growing up. Depending on where you squirted the milk on the inside of the pail, you'd get a different note. We'd play songs, and the other person would have to guess what they were.

Though Janice had come upon the term *savant* in one of her courses, it hadn't really stuck with her. "There was this dinky little paragraph about savant syndrome in one of my textbooks," she said, "but the term was *idiot savant,* and I just passed that right by." She would soon come to learn, however, that Tony and others like him are special in a way that cannot be expressed in medical terminology. They are, in many ways, beyond words.

Chapter Three

ISLANDS *of* GENIUS:
THE MYSTERY *of*
SAVANT SYNDROME

"Until we can explain the savant,
we cannot explain ourselves."

—*Darold A. Treffert, MD*

PRODIGIOUS SAVANTS SUCH AS TONY, whose special skills would be extraordinary even in a non-disabled person, are exceedingly rare. Such an individual, who embodies the extremes of cognitive disability and musical genius, evokes awe in everyone he meets. Darold A. Treffert, MD, one of Tony's great admirers and a leading expert on savant syndrome, first learned of Tony when Janice sent him medical records, videos, and other documentation about Tony's behavioral and musical development in the late 1980s. In 1991, Dr. Treffert met Tony in person for an interview for NBC's *Today Show,* and he has been a friend of the family ever since.

Dr. Treffert, who is a psychiatrist at St. Agnes Hospital in Fond du Lac, Wisconsin, and a clinical professor at the University of Wisconsin Medical School, has spent more than four decades studying savant syndrome. He met his first savant on his first day on the job in a child's psychiatric unit in 1962, and since then he has devoted much of his research and study to the field. The same curiosity about the unknown that drew him to psychiatry led him to delve into savant syndrome in particular, convinced that the condition can not only be explained but can also teach us a great deal about memory and human potential. "We cannot simply look at the savant in wonderment and awe, then go on as if no explanation is due, or none possible," Dr. Treffert wrote in his book, *Extraordinary People: Understanding Savant Syndrome.* "Savant syndrome may be difficult to explain, but surely it cannot be unexplainable."

In an interview in 2004, Dr. Treffert stated that "at the present time, there are really three musical savants I am aware of where improvisation, particularly jazz, is their specialty." He lists these as Tony DeBlois; Derek Paravicini, a pianist who lives in London; and Matt Savage, a young pianist from New Hampshire. Another musical savant whom Dr. Treffert puts alongside these three as sharing the extremely rare ability to create music rather than merely repeat it is Hikari Oe, a Japanese savant who composes classical music.

For Dr. Treffert, the lessons of Tony DeBlois and other savants are opening new doors of understanding about amazing talents that may lie within each of us. He theorizes that everyone possesses extraordinary latent abilities that we may one day be able to access through a pathway other than brain injury or some other neurological disability. When we fully understand the savant, according to Dr. Treffert, we can tap into what he calls our "inner savant," or the Rain Man within each of us. (Dr. Treffert was the expert consultant on the film *Rain Man,* starring Dustin Hoffman, who portrayed a mathematical savant.)

As Dr. Treffert explains, not all savants have autism, and not all people with autism are savants. The syndrome appears in people with some sort of developmental disability, which can be due to autism, mental retardation, or damage to the central nervous system from injury or disease. Following is a summary of well-established facts about savant syndrome:

• Approximately 10 percent of people with autism have some level of savant skills.

- About 1 percent of people with other types of developmental disabilities show savant skills.
- Savant abilities are limited to five basic areas: music, art, calendar calculating, math calculating, and mechanical or spatial skills.
- Music is the most common savant skill, usually expressed by playing piano by ear and with perfect pitch; the second most common ability is art.
- Most savants are male; there are six male savants to every one female savant.
- Savants possess phenomenal memory within the narrow focus of their special ability; instant access to the deepest levels of memory is an integral part of the syndrome.
- Neurological damage from brain injury or dementia can result in the sudden acquisition of savant skills in a previously nondisabled person.

The first detailed, classic medical description of savant syndrome was given by British psychiatrist J. Langdon Down, MD, in a series of lectures in 1887. He spoke about patients diagnosed as "idiot savants," a term he coined but eventually tried to soften by replacing "idiot" with "feebleminded," which at the time did not sound as condescending as it does now. Dr. Down's brief initial description of these patients, who he had observed closely for thirty years, was that of "children who, while feebleminded, exhibit special faculties, which are capable of being cultivated to a very great extent." Dr. Down is best remembered for his description of a type of mental retardation that now bears his name, Down syndrome; but he contributed valuable insights into savant syndrome with these lectures, which were eventually published in a textbook about developmental disabilities.

Dr. Down described cases of children who could memorize dates, seemingly endless lists of historical events, and entire books. One boy, for example, could recite *The Rise and Fall of the Roman Empire* word for word but without understanding the content. He even repeated verbatim the mistake he made in skipping one line, always interrupting himself in the same place to make the correction exactly as he had done the first time. Dr. Down created the term *verbal adhesion* for this form of unconscious mimicking behavior, which is a prominent aspect of savant syndrome. Other boys (Dr. Down never met a female savant in his entire career) could perform mathematical calculations instantly, such as the twelve-year-old who could multiply any three-digit number by another three-digit number as quickly as writing it down, with perfect accuracy. Some savants could tell time with perfect precision without using a clock, and others showed perfect accuracy in memorizing music.

After hearing a song or an entire opera just once, these children could hum or sing the pieces down to the exact word and pitch forever afterward.

Music is the most common form of genius expressed in savants, and the most famous case in American history comes from the Civil War period, about twenty years before Dr. Down made his famous lectures in London. Thomas Greene Bethune, or Blind Tom, came to live on a Georgia plantation when his mother was sold at a slave auction to a Colonel Bethune in 1850. Tom was included in the purchase at no cost because he was blind and severely disabled both physically and mentally. He did not speak, could barely walk, was restless and flew into rages, and showed no interest in anything except the music he heard in the parlor as the colonel's daughters played their sonatas and piano duets. The colonel was astonished to come downstairs late one night, wakened by the strains of a Mozart sonata, to find four-year-old Tom seated at the piano playing the piece perfectly. One of the girls had been practicing the piece for weeks before mastering it, and Tom played the final version with complete confidence and flair. The family soon learned that Tom could play anything perfectly after just one hearing, and the colonel hired several professional musicians to play score after score for Tom to build his repertoire. Finally, at age seven, Tom's reputation prompted the colonel to schedule a concert, and it was a sellout. From there, Tom went on the road and began a tour that earned one hundred thousand dollars in ticket sales the first year.

Although Blind Tom's vocabulary was limited to about one hundred words, his musical repertoire consisted of about five thousand pieces by Bach, Beethoven, Mendelssohn, Chopin, Verdi, and many others. At age eleven he played for President James Buchanan at the White House, followed by a world tour at age sixteen. Newspaper descriptions of his performance portray a bizarre physical component of Tom's listening process. One writer described his "studying posture" as a pirouette-like stance, in which he stood on one leg with the other horizontal to the floor. He spun around in this "T" position as he listened to a new piece of music, sometimes flapping his hands or stopping to hold the position for a moment before proceeding to spin again. Following this, Tom went to the piano and flawlessly played the piece he had just heard. He introduced himself in the third person, "Tom will now play . . . " and, following each piece, he joined the audience in gleeful applause, clapping his hands in a childlike way from the piano bench.

Over the years, many people tested Tom's ability by asking him to play newly written pieces that he could not possibly have heard before, which he played as perfectly as all the others after just one hearing. The most astonishing results came when a composer brought a fourteen-page piano duet to the piano, which of course Tom could neither see nor read. The composer sat on the right side of the bench to play the primo part, and Tom sat next to him to play the secondo. In perfect rhythm and time, Tom improvised a brilliant secondo accompaniment while the composer played the primo part. After that, he forced the composer off the bench and played the primo part that he had miraculously memorized while playing the secondo.

Blind Tom was a star in his day, often described as the eighth wonder of the world. At one point, a panel of musicians signed an official statement about Tom's remarkable contributions to music: "Whether in his improvisations of performances of compositions by Gottschalk, Verdi, and others, in fact in every form of musical examination—and the experiments are too numerous to mention—he showed a capacity ranking him among the most wonderful phenomena in musical history."

There have been only about one hundred prodigious savants like Blind Tom in recorded history, and joining these ranks is another pianist who gained fame with his remarkable talent about one hundred years later. Leslie

Lemke was born premature in Milwaukee, Wisconsin, in 1952 and put up for adoption at birth. He was taken in by a fifty-two-year-old nurse named May Lemke, who had already raised five children. She and her husband lovingly cared for the baby, who was blind, brain damaged, and suffering from cerebral palsy. Leslie loved music; and at age fourteen, his genius came to light when he sat down at the piano to play Tchaikovsky's Piano Concerto no. 1, which he had just heard as the soundtrack to a film the Lemkes had watched on television. Knowing that performing gave Leslie great joy, May set up concerts for him at fairs and churches. When news spread about his talent, he became the subject of stories on television such as the *CBS Evening News* with Walter Cronkite. Leslie went on to tour throughout the United States and the world, and he played to a twelve-hundred-person audience in Appleton as recently as October 2003. Dr. Treffert, who attended that concert, was moved to describe the personal dimension that took precedence over his physician's viewpoint that night, reminding him that at the heart of the savant story is the story of selfless, loving caregivers.

On a personal level, during this remarkable concert experience, my scientific interest in synapses and circuits was overshadowed and superceded by the human interest that Leslie Lemke's story generates in terms of his unique person and potential, and in terms of how often families, like his, unselfishly and proudly go forward filling the special needs of their loved one, relishing and focusing so zealously those talents, attributes, and abilities that are present even if some other skills are absent or compromised.

Dr. Treffert was moved in the same way when he met Tony and his family in 1991. "I had seen some of his playing on videotape," he said, "but that's no substitute for being there in person, like watching the Packers play on television is no substitute for being at the stadium. It's an awe-inspiring kind of experience when you see that kind of ability." Dr. Treffert was struck by Tony's friendliness and outgoing nature, which was unusual for an autistic person, at least for the many that he had met and worked with through the years. "He was much more outgoing than I had imagined him to be in terms of being able to feel comfortable, to dialog, to sit down and chat," Dr. Treffert recalled. "Sometimes, when you try to interview a savant, it's difficult because there's not much feedback, not much participation, but with Tony I thought we hit it off pretty well; we chatted." Tony was much more comfortable socially than Dr. Treffert had expected; and when Dr. Treffert met Janice, he recognized the devotion and unconditional love that played a part in that social ease. He had seen this in May Lemke and other parents of prodigious savants, people who did not hold regrets about what their child lacked but who rejoiced in what they had—in the totality of the child, of which their rare talent was only one part. "In totality, certainly, Tony's music is spectacular; but there's much more of a gleam in Janice's eye about Tony as a person, not just about what he does," said Dr. Treffert. "Behind each of these prodigious savants, at least where they've really excelled, is this family acceptance, which I think is a vital part of the equation."

Dr. Treffert describes this equation of factors found in savant syndrome as a triad consisting of, one, a particular type of brain circuitry; two, the obsessive practice of a particular talent; and three, the positive reinforcement of a loving parent or other caregiver. An attempt to understand the first factor, the neurological aspect, is made by a group of theories about what occurs in the savant brain. One prominent theory suggests that left-hemispheric damage prompts the right hemisphere to compensate. The functions of the left hemisphere are speech and language, logical and analytical thinking, perceiving time, manual skills, and recognizing letters, words, and numbers. Right hemisphere functions include intuition, facial movements and body language, creativity, spatial awareness, mathematical operations, and recognizing faces, places, and objects. When the left hemisphere is damaged, the right hemisphere assumes more activity, and its functions become more pronounced. Brain scans reveal that savants have left-hemisphere dysfunction, which provides the hard science behind this theory.

Although the left-brain/right-brain concept is useful for understanding some of the brain's basic functions, research shows that several aspects of music perception are processed all over the brain. Even though some processes, such as reading music, appear to be located in the right hemisphere, the musical brain has been described as "modularized," with each component of musical experience processed by different neural pathways in the left/right, front/back, and top/bottom regions of the brain. These independent modules include separate areas for perceiving melody and rhythm, for example, and music is now understood to be a unique mode of knowing that is completely separate from language and other types of cognitive processes. Emotion, the most immediate experience of music for both performers and listeners, is the least understood in terms of neurology.

Another theory about savant brain circuitry that relates to this whole-brain perspective of musical neural pathways proposes that the right hemisphere does not actually increase its functioning but is simply freed from the overwhelming dominance of the left hemisphere. The left hemisphere is dominant in our species because of language development, and this "release of tyranny" theory suggests that the right brain—normally over-shadowed by this dominance—is allowed to come to the forefront with its innate abilities.

Tony's neurological reports reveal that, like all savants, he has left-hemispheric damage. A CT scan (computerized tomography or CAT scan) taken when he was eight years old revealed "mild cerebral atrophy of the left hemisphere . . . [with] a normal amount of tissue in the right hemisphere and decreased in the left." The report concluded that "the findings . . . do suggest an organic basis for Anthony's problems."

In a clinical assessment written in 1989, Dr. Treffert described Tony's neurological condition as follows:

> *As is the case with other savants, he shows, on CT scan, left hemisphere damage with right hemisphere com-pensation and with that characteristic phenomenon, a prestigious right hemisphere skill (music) along with markedly enhanced habit memory. He demonstrates thoroughly and convincingly the astonishing paradox of mental handicap with extraordinary functioning in some limited areas, which is the savant syndrome.*

Another theory that has emerged in the past few years targets problems with the corpus callosum, which connects the two hemispheres of the brain. Some scientists believe that damage to the corpus callosum accounts for the narrowing of focus in autistic children. Brain scans reveal that an autistic person tends to have a smaller corpus callosum, which inhibits communication between the hemispheres and may promote a narrow focus on one particular brain function. This connectivity theory explains an autistic child's obsessive craving for sameness and repeated activity.

Related to the left-brain/right-brain issues of savant syndrome is the finding of an important study by Harvard neurologists Norman Geschwind, MD, and Albert Galaburda, MD, published in the mid-1980s. Their study provided an explanation for the higher incidence of savant syndrome in males than in females and also supported the left-side damage/right-side compensation theory of savant syndrome. According to these scientists, the left hemisphere develops later than the right in the fetus and is therefore susceptible to prenatal chemical influences for a longer time. The male fetus produces high quantities of testosterone during its development, and this hormone can slow the growth and impair the functioning of the vulnerable left hemisphere. As a result, the right hemisphere compensates with more growth and development, and males usually have slightly larger right hemispheres than females. The potential for damage to the left hemisphere from exposure to testosterone explains why savant syndrome—as well as other central nervous system dysfunctions, such as autism and dyslexia—is more common in males.

In addition to the left-hemisphere issue, the neurological uniqueness of savants involves their mysterious access to deep memory. While most people learn through their everyday conscious memory, called *cognitive memory*, savants store information in a deeper level of circuitry called *noncognitive* or *habit memory*. Information stored in this part of the brain is accessed as an automatic response to a certain stimulus rather than as a process of thinking. For example, this is the memory we use when we're driving, which tells our muscles how to steer while our cognitive memory is busy thinking about our day or talking on the cell phone. When a musical savant like Tony listens to music, the information is stored in the habit memory pathway, and his unique type of access to that memory allows him to tap into it automatically. Dr. Treffert describes the savant memory as "a highly developed, compensatory, noncognitive, alternative pathway developed to compensate for injury to or absence of the more usual and more frequently used cognitive memory seen in the rest of us."

Much more is known about cognitive memory than about habit memory. Savants cannot explain how they access the answers to mathematical problems, pick out the day of the week of a specific date two hundred years ago, or recall, note for note, complex musical pieces. The retrieval is unconscious and automatic. Another theoretical concept of memory that may be involved in the savant's ability to utilize this deep level of the neurological system involves ancestral or genetic memory. Swiss psychiatrist Carl Jung coined the term *collective unconscious* to describe the repository of memory that is shared by the entire human race. This memory reveals itself in the common myths, symbols, and stories that cultures share throughout the world and throughout history.

Dr. Treffert's ideas about this realm of memory take a more "hard science" slant as he attempts to apply it to the mystique of the savant. Comparing the brain's memory system to a computer, he refers to information as software: "I've come to believe in the collective unconscious not as psychological myths that are handed down by generations but as actual wiring, instinctual, which I call software installed. It's clear that some of these prodigious savants are knowing things they cannot have learned. It had to come installed." Dr. Treffert believes that this aspect of the complex territory of human memory may be hidden from most of us most of the time simply as a survival mechanism—too much information would make our lives too complex.

This level of memory may also explain why it appears that we come with tons of software installed that we don't use. It's not because we're lazy but because it would cause the same situation as when I try to use all my software on my computer at the same time—it would crash. It's almost as if some of these chips have a survival value to us if something happens to us. I think we tend to look at ourselves as being born with a tremendous piece of hardware, the brain, and a blank slate, and we become what we put on this disk. But I think savants come with this installed and they have access to it that we don't.

Supporting this concept that we all possess a seemingly limitless store of information and skills, but not the wiring to access it, is the fascinating discovery that this access can be acquired. Scientists have witnessed savant skills emerge in people who experience left-brain injury from stroke, disease, dementia, or other ailments. One study from 1998, for example, reported the sudden onset of highly sophisticated artistic skills in five older adults who suffered from dementia. These patients became obsessed with creating meticulous, exact renditions of visual images on a canvas; their new memory access also allowed them to recreate a scene down to the minutest detail, months after observing it.

The big question is, of course, can we learn to access these unique savantlike pathways in a way other than brain damage? A remarkable study done by two researchers in the psychiatry department at the University of Oklahoma in 1978 hints that this is a possibility. The researchers had been studying two renowned calendar-calculating savants, identical twins from New York named George and Charles. They could tell you, for example, the day of the week for dates going back as far as the year 1700. The researchers set up an experiment involving a one-page table of dates that was given to a graduate student named Benj Langdon. This grid represented a slice of the information that the twins could automatically access at any time, and the researchers sought to discover whether this automatic access could be developed by a typical person. A journalist described the results in an article in *Psychology Today*.

Langdon practiced night and day, trying to develop a high degree of proficiency at some rather complex calculations that involved memorizing a one-page table. Langdon became quite good at the calculating. But despite an enormous amount of practice, he could not match the speed of the twins for quite a long time.

Then suddenly, he discovered he could match their speed. Quite to Langdon's surprise, his brain had somehow automated the complex calculations; it had absorbed the table to be memorized so efficiently that now calendar calculating was second nature to him; he no longer had to consciously go through the various operations.

After a long, relentless struggle, Langdon's brain had developed the pathway that is such an integral facct of savant syndrome; and in so doing, it opened up the possibility that this pathway can be learned. Most people are shielded from access to this deepest memory field, but Langdon's experience confirms that there are vast horizons of human potential awaiting to be discovered.

Dr. Treffert remarked that autistic behavior may reveal why this shield has been so carefully constructed in the normal brain: "Autism, especially in its very severe form, may be the overwhelming of all of these memory chips which they can't sort out. It's like a television set that doesn't have a tuner. Autistics are bombarded by all this stuff, and they can't sort it out."

❧ While brain physiology makes up the first aspect of the triad of savant syndrome, the second part involves the skill itself and the savant's obsessive relationship to it.

Whether expressed as mathematical calculating, calendar calculating, or artistic or musical skill, the talent takes over the life of the person. Savants are unilateral in their interests, and their day revolves around their particular skill. "The unique nature and almost forcefulness of this obsessiveness makes the savant's talent as much of a force as a gift," said Dr. Treffert. "They have to play; they have to practice; they have to calculate."

The third part of the phenomenon is the family or caregiver who provides a safe, loving, nurturing haven for the savant. Positive reinforcement, praise, and unconditional acceptance are vital to creating an environment in which savants are able to thrive and develop closer relationships to their families and interact with the world. Everyone likes positive feedback, of course, but the emotional needs of savants are as unique as their gifts.

The neurology of the savant, like that of the autistic person, includes more limited access to the emotional centers of the brain. Parents of savants express their love and give reinforcement often without the benefit of the typical feedback that a child gives in response to affection. Praise and encouragement increase the savant's self-esteem and add joy to his or her life. This joy is evident during Tony's performances, for example, when he claps along with the audience after a piece, grins, and asks, "Isn't it good?"

Some people have criticized the practice of putting musical savants onstage as a form of exploitation. But it is difficult for others to put this negative connotation on the experience when it clearly brings so much joy to the performer. Tony, like other musical savants, does not suffer from performance anxiety; he never gets nervous before a performance. "It isn't exploitation because Tony loves applause and a satisfied audience," said Dr. Treffert. "It's tremendously reinforcing. The quality of that sort of reinforcement and the family's investment in it is terribly important."

While savant syndrome encompasses the three elements of brain dysfunction, obsessive behavior with the skill, and nurturing support, another triad comes to light specifically in terms of the musical savant. Throughout the literature, from Blind Tom to the current day, the condition of the musical savant entails the three elements of blindness, cognitive difficulty, and musical genius.

In Tony's case, blindness occurred as a result of oxygen therapy that kept him alive as a premature infant, while Leslie Lemke's blindness was the result of glaucoma in infancy. Cognitive difficulty, in Tony's case, is the result of brain lesions that show up on his CT scan, but the left-hemisphere dysfunctions of musical savants have also been the result of accidental injury and other causes.

The source of musical genius, surprisingly, does not come from an obvious genetic inheritance; the literature does not contain family histories in which the savant was born into a musically gifted family, as is often the case with musical prodigies. Tony's mother played the clarinet in school, and her siblings also played musical instruments in junior high, but they do not consider themselves musically gifted, nor have they played their instruments since that time.

The triad of blindness, cognitive disability, and musical genius shows up with uncanny regularity in musical savants, although the interrelationship of these three elements is not yet clear. Their appearance in the musical savant is one of the ongoing mysteries of the syndrome that physicians such as Dr. Treffert continue to ponder and study.

The old adage states that we utilize only 10 percent of our brains, and savants remind us of this fact with startling clarity. The insights about brain hemisphere functions and memory that come out of savant research are expanding our ideas about who we are and what we are capable of. For Dr. Treffert, one of the most valuable benefits of this knowledge is a new appreciation for right-brain functions that we have tended to dismiss as frivolous or unessential compared with work, relationships, and other aspects of our day-to-day lives. As a start, he observes that corporations have begun to value the visionary qualities of the right brain. This is evidenced by the popularity of Betty Edwards, PhD,'s weeklong workshops based on her book, *New Drawing on the Right Side of the Brain*, which offers methods for slowing down left-hemisphere dominance in order to release right-hemisphere abilities.

In the business world, these abilities include seeing the big picture and solving problems from a more creative, holistic perspective. "It's interesting," said Dr. Treffert, "that up until a few years ago, when most of the organizations went looking for a CEO, they looked for a good left-hemisphere management-by-objectives kind of person. Now, they're saying they want someone with vision, and that's really a right-brain skill."

The issue of practical versus artistic, right-brain skills came up in Tony's experience at various schools, where well-intentioned educators and occupational therapists thought it was more important for him to learn how to feed himself, tie his shoes, and learn vocabulary than to play the piano. But Dr. Treffert believes that Tony's music is his pathway to learning language and other skills and that allowing him to develop his gifts opens up a "conduit to normalization" that is the unique pathway of the savant. In a clinical assessment, Dr. Treffert described this conduit as essential to Tony's development.

The musical gift that Anthony DeBlois shows is more than a curious and conspicuous talent. Like other savants, in his case it can be the conduit to further socialization, amelioration of some of his autistic symptoms, and a mechanism to raise considerably whatever hindrances his basic mental handicap produce. While continual attention to the specific talent of the savant may at times seem optional or even frivolous, it is through training that talent that the savant can move beyond the defect toward better attention to daily living skills, enhanced socialization, better communication skills, more interactive relationships, and even intimacy. . . .

Such skills become a mode of expression through which others can reach and interact with the savant, and consequently those skills lead to the development of other related skills and human communication. The skills serve as a window to the world for the savant, and they serve as a window to the savant for the rest of us.

This practical aspect of Tony's musical genius echoes the practical functions of studying savant syndrome to enhance science's understanding of the brain. But Dr. Treffert is quick to point out that attempting to understand the physiology of the syndrome as a scientist in no way takes away from the miraculous nature of the condition, one that inspires awe at the mysteries of nature. Dr. Treffert believes that savant syndrome must be understood in order to fully understand the brain and the human mind and that no model of cognition or behavior is complete without incorporating the unique pathways of the savant.

Even when science reaches this understanding, Dr. Treffert believes that there will still be plenty of room for wonder at the complexity of it. "I still marvel at it, I'm still in awe of it, but it's no different than the phenomenon of a miraculous medical recovery and eventually finding the underlying cause. The body's ability to do what it did can still be considered miraculous. You don't detract from the miracle by trying to understand how it happened."

Chapter Four

"A BRAIN LIKE *a* TAPE RECORDER"

"It is highly likely that savant skills differ
considerably in their social consequences.
In this respect, the musical savant probably
has a significant advantage. Music has
expressive and communicative qualities
that are readily appreciated by others
and performing music provides
a means of contact with others."

—*Leon K. Miller,* Musical Savants

Antonia Felix: Do you get nervous before you play?

Tony DeBlois: No! I feel excited before I go onstage. When we do a big concert, I just really get my whole adrenaline excited up there.

Antonia: Do you have a favorite musician that you like to listen to? A favorite CD?

Tony: My favorite CD is my jazz vocal CD with me singing with the Winiker band. Bo plays trumpet on the CD. He's my trumpet teacher. Isn't it great? I like the Johnny Mercer CD, all the Johnny Mercer songs.

Antonia: Next to the piano, what is your favorite instrument?

Tony: Trumpet, latest one was the saxophone. And the next one after that is the oboe. I've heard it in the Boston Symphony Orchestra on the radio. I've heard a lot of great musicians that play oboe on stage. Actually, my favorite evening show on Channel Two is Great Performances. I like classical music because it has trumpet in it [hums the theme to *Masterpiece Theatre*].

Antonia: I know you do performances in schools. What do you like about it?

Tony: I love doing it; it's so fun. I get so excited working with the students. My favorite part is when, after a while, the students get to ask me some questions. A lot of long ones. Isn't it great? My favorite question is, "How many hours do you practice during the day?" I tell them it's okay to be different, be yourself. The most important words are thank you; the three Ps are practice, practice, practice.

Antonia: Did you like being with your fellow students at Berklee?

Tony: I liked them all. I also liked my piano teacher, Suzanna Sifter. I enjoyed meeting . . . you know who I also liked? Sharon Brown [voice teacher]. I really liked Sharon Brown. My favorite part of going to Berklee was the senior recital toward the end of the year. Each of the students gets to perform. I was one of them. I got up to the stage, and a big audience was clapping for me. The students gave me a standing ovation. I'd never met Patti LaBelle before.

Antonia: Were you proud to go onstage and get that diploma?

Tony: Exciting. Well, I got all A's in my homework, and I got all my grades. I went into the learning lab and turned in my homework on disc to the teacher, and the teacher gave me an A. I earned an A for turning in my exams. Adam was my aide, and he helped me with my homework.

We walked into the learning lab before lunch. Isn't that great? I used to have a lunch schedule. Twelve o'clock when class got out. We went to Little Stevie's right across from the 150 building. Actually, my favorite pizza was the cheese pizza, right, Mom? I always get a soda. They were a buck a slice. One time, I met my girlfriend at Dunkin' Donuts. As I was walking over to class one year, someone said hello to me as I went inside the door, and I said, "I have to run to class right now."

Antonia: You travel a lot to perform. What's fun about going on road trips with Mom?

Tony: My favorite part of the road trip is watching TV while we're on the road. Mom and I like to watch *Law & Order* when we're on road trips. When we're stopping at a motel. My favorite part was, going to work, making sure I get paid, actually. Make sure I get my money. And I get my paycheck. You know what I do? I like going to the ATM and depositing the money. They always say, "Here's the check for Tony DeBlois." Isn't it great? They used to put the check in the mail. They always hand me an envelope with the money in it. I like it in an envelope, right? I say, "Envelope please," like the Academy Awards.

Antonia: Do you think you make people happy at your concerts?

Tony: I do, yes. When we do a lot of the jazz music, yes. For instance, when we did play at, like, Skipjack's, you are always surprised. After I finish a solo on the piano, they always clap for me. Wasn't that great? I really like playing with the Winikers. Bill and Bo are so great. We really team up together, me and Bill and Bo. Maybe they should go on the road with us, the Winiker guys. I sort of thought of that idea, do a tour in different cities—isn't it good?

Antonia: Do you like to sign autographs for your fans?

Tony: I like to autograph CDs. I autograph all my CDs. I like the CD sales. I get to go out and sell CDs. Isn't that great? When people go to my Web site, they'll look at my pictures, they'll look at my CDs. Once people take the CDs home, they listen to [them] and they go, "You've got to hear this." I'm always taking CD orders over the phone. I say to Mom, "They want a CD order."

Antonia: Does music have a feeling inside you?

Tony: It feels very special. When I play good music on the piano. Especially when I say "The Wind Beneath My Wings" and I dedicate it to my mom. That's what I sing when I go out to the schools. "Thank you, thank you, thank God for Mom, the wind beneath my wings." Then she comes over and gives me a kiss and a hug.

⟜ Tony was three years old when Janice and Owen discovered that Janice was pregnant again. As it had the previous time, Janice's intuition told her that this baby would go to term and would survive; and in the spring of 1977, she continued her studies at El Paso Community College with renewed excitement about having another child. She also remained active in many organizations related to her education and to Tony's care. She served on the Ways and Means Committee of the Texas Association of the Deaf, Blind, and Multiply Handicapped and served as president of the El Paso Community College Childcare Cooperative. Throughout her pregnancy, she also continued to attend events such as a parent-teacher training conference for the deaf-blind, a Department of Public Welfare workshop, and a regional conference on the rights of the handicapped.

Owen's service in the US Army was up in 1977, and

like Janice, he became a full-time student on the GI Bill. They each arranged their schedules to share the responsibility of caring for Tony when he wasn't in daycare. In his free time, Owen often visited one of his professors in the anthropology department who was building an adobe house in an isolated area outside of Socorro, Texas, about fifteen miles southeast of El Paso. Much to Janice's surprise, Owen had developed quite a wanderlust, and he often talked about building a log cabin in Alaska, where regions were still open for homesteading. His professor friend was living that dream—the hippie Texan version—by building a round adobe house with dirt floors and living off the land in Socorro. When Janice's parents came down for a visit that May, Owen drove them all out there to show them the property, and he talked about building his own rustic place next to his friend's house one day.

On July 29, Janice underwent a scheduled Cesarean section at Thomason General Hospital in El Paso. This procedure was necessary because she had delivered baby Aaron by Cesarean section. Because of Janice's history with previous pregnancies and with Tony's emergency needs at his birth, her doctor arranged to have the neonatal intensive care unit ready. Janice had declined an amniocentesis test during this pregnancy because she would not consider aborting the baby if they uncovered any type of problem, so the doctors were alert for any problems with the delivery. The Cesarean surgery went smoothly, and at 8:22 a.m. on July 29, 1977, Ralph Mooney was born.

Ralph was a full-term baby weighing eight pounds, two ounces, but from the first moment the obstetrician knew there was something wrong. Ralph struggled to breathe, and the team rushed him to the neonatal intensive care unit. After Janice awoke from the anesthesia, she was stunned to find out that her baby was in intensive care.

The next day, Janice's doctor informed her that the baby might need open-heart surgery. He asked her to sign a transfer order to move Ralph to the Providence Memorial Hospital in El Paso, where they had the staff and facilities to do the surgery on an infant. Janice had hoped that Ralph could go to the neonatal ward at the William Beaumont Army Medical Center, where Tony had received such outstanding care; but because both Janice and Owen were out of the army, they were no longer eligible to go to the military hospital. During the ambulance ride, Ralph's breathing improved, and by the time he got to Providence, the doctor was able to rule out surgery. He believed that some of the movement in the ambulance had loosened a mucous plug that had blocked Ralph's airway.

Although heart problems were ruled out, Ralph still needed to stay in intensive care for close observation of his respiratory functioning. He required oxygen therapy during the five weeks he spent in the hospital. Unlike Tony, whose body absorbed too much oxygen in his first weeks, Ralph's body could not absorb enough. Ralph's respiratory problems brought back a flood of memories in Janice and Owen about Tony's traumatic earliest months. Would the new baby's problems lead to developmental challenges as Tony's had? It was too early to tell, but Ralph was a sick baby in those first weeks.

Janice was released from the hospital in five days and finally got to drive over to Providence to see Ralph. About five days later, however, she developed a high fever and was readmitted to Thomason with a uterine infection. She spent the next ten days confined to her hospital bed to receive a drip of antibiotics. One of the memories imprinted on her mind from those weeks was the news shocker of August 1977—the death of Elvis Presley—which was forever linked in her mind to the Spanish verb conjugations she studied during her stay for her summer intensive Spanish course. Janice kept up with the class with the help of a tutor provided by El Paso Community College, and she spent hours each day studying while the television played in the background. "The King is dead" . . . *¡Oh mi dios, el Rey es muerto!*

The Mooneys were anxious to see Tony's reaction when they brought baby Ralph home for the first time. His reaction was quite unusual.

Janice's Journal

When we brought Ralph home, I sat down with him on the floor and let Tony touch him. In spite of everything people think after seeing movies about Helen Keller, blind people don't go around touching faces to find out what someone feels like. Tony just touched him here and there for a few seconds. We talked all through it, told him all about the baby, but he was in his own world; it didn't impress him any. The only time we realized that Tony knew that Ralph existed was when he crawled over to his crib, reached in, and pressed his head. This made Ralph cry out, and every once in a while Tony would seem to try to "sneak" into his room, crawling quietly, in order to touch Ralph's head and make him make noise. We figured that Tony thought Ralph was a toy.

Janice was overjoyed to have two babies, even though she had her hands full between an infant, a blind and disabled three-year-old, and college classes. There were twice as many toys under the tree that Christmas; and like Janice, Owen was happy with his classes and spent plenty of quality time with the boys. Although the children made them very happy, Tony was also the source of the only disagreements Owen and Janice seemed to have.

Everything Janice had learned about autism led her to believe that the most effective route for dealing with Tony was a behavior modification approach. This method—defining a clear goal behavior, giving a specific command as the stimulus, observing the results, and offering a praise reward if the correct behavior is performed—continues to be the most popular way of working with autistic children. Owen, however, thought that behavior modification was "for animals in zoos." And sometimes he did not share Janice's patience in working on the repetitive, basic tasks that she believed were essential to Tony's development. When Janice sat down with Tony to teach him how to string beads, for example, Owen would roll his eyes and say, "Boring!" Janice felt that they had to figure out how to work together on this, not only for Tony's well-being but also for the emotional stability of both boys. Her early childhood training had taught her about the deep repercussions of growing up in a home filled with the tension of parents arguing, and she didn't want to expose her boys to that. She believed that she and Owen would work it out; they had been through a lot together, and they could get through this.

By the time Ralph was six months old, Janice had settled into her new routine as a mother of two, and she looked forward to finishing her last set of courses at the university. But something was brewing in the background, out of her sight, that would cause the world she thought was relatively stable and secure to come crashing down around her. After folding the laundry one day, Janice went to the bedroom and opened Owen's top dresser drawer to put away his socks. The drawer was empty. She pulled open the rest of the drawers—also empty—and found that all of his clothes were cleared out of the closet. He was gone, and she hadn't seen it coming. They had disagreed about how to work with Tony, but these discussions had never escalated into a fight or hinted that they had turned a corner in their relationship. As far as Janice was concerned, she and Owen were closer than ever, and she searched her mind for hints that she'd missed.

Janice suspected that Owen had gone to his friend's place in Socorro, and when he didn't return in a few days, she drove out there hoping to either find him or ask his friends if they knew where he was. Owen was there, as she expected, living in a "dwelling" that he had built and that he was very proud to show her. To Janice it looked like nothing more than a hole in the ground covered with a flap of corrugated metal for a roof. Owen had left because he wanted to explore a new lifestyle, but he told Janice that he would come home often to be with the children.

Though Owen soon gave up on the hole in the ground and moved into a house about five blocks away from Janice, he stayed true to his commitment to Tony and Ralph as a devoted father. But Janice and Owen both agreed that the marriage was over, and they separated.

✦ Financially, Janice was okay. The monthly check she received from the GI Bill was more than enough to take care of the rent (her three-bedroom house was only $120 a month), her low quarterly tuition, groceries, day-care, and incidentals. During her last year at the university, Janice also earned a small salary as a teacher at St. Pius X School, a Catholic elementary school in El Paso. She enrolled in even more classes per semester after Ralph was born, to speed up her date of graduation. Because of the slower pace with which she had begun her triple major, she would not be set to graduate until 1981.

While at the university, Janice researched schools for the blind throughout the country that would provide the best possible situation for Tony. With a degree and some teaching experience, she hoped she would be able to find a good job in whatever city that school was located. She first learned about the Perkins School for the Blind in Watertown, Massachusetts, in one of her classes, and she was struck by the statement in one source that it was "the oldest school for the blind in the free world and the third oldest in the world." That fact alone, Janice figured, revealed that they had been teaching blind children longer than anyone else, and she immediately called the school to get more information. Perkins's location a few miles west of Boston was also attractive because being in a major metropolitan area would increase her chances of finding a teaching job.

Tony's special needs were not Janice's only concern. By the time Ralph was two, it was obvious that his language was not developing normally. Shortly after Ralph's third birthday, he was evaluated by a school psychiatrist with the El Paso school district, who confirmed that Ralph was language delayed. He also reported that Ralph's IQ was 129, which school administrators felt was far too high to qualify him for special education preschool programs. Janice knew that Ralph would benefit from small class groups with specially trained instructors, and she also knew that the law was on her side. But until she could solve this dispute with the school district, she worked with Ralph at home, using the language development skills she had learned at El Paso Community College and in working with Tony.

Ralph's development problems were eventually diagnosed as Asperger's syndrome, a neurological disorder in which the child has normal intelligence but also a range of autistic-like behaviors. These behaviors can include a preoccupation with one particular interest; obsessive routines; deficiencies in social skills; hypersensitivity to sounds, smells, and other stimuli; and an unusual use of language. Ralph's IQ, which falls into the high intelligence range (50 percent of the population has IQ scores between 90 and 110; Einstein's IQ was 160), is another common factor in Asperger's: Many of these children have high intelligence and rich vocabularies but have a difficult time using language socially. Asperger's syndrome also involves asocial, autistic-like behaviors such as a lack of interest in making friends, avoidance of eye contact, and an inability to interpret or use body language. The syndrome—which is named after Viennese physician Hans Asperger, who published a paper about the disorder in 1944—is sometimes described as *high functioning autism*. Before the diagnosis entered the medical mainstream, many such people were simply considered eccentric, socially inept, and physically clumsy.

In his teens, Ralph was diagnosed with another disorder that further explained his language problems and his difficulty in learning to read. A blood workup revealed that he has Klinefelter's syndrome, a condition that results from having an extra X chromosome. The XXY chromosome arrangement is not uncommon; it can occur in one in five hundred to one in one thousand male births, and only a minority of XXY babies grow up to develop some of the symptoms associated with Klinefelter's syndrome. Those who do, like Ralph, experience a range of physical and psychological traits including sparse facial and body hair, infertility, a shy and passive disposition in early childhood that remains consistent through adulthood, and slow speech and language development.

Although Ralph's developmental problems were not as severe as Tony's, he was clearly a special-needs child who required specialized education and therapies. Janice had to consider this when choosing a new home for her family, and the more she learned about the Perkins School and the Boston area, the better it sounded. By the time Janice graduated from the university in 1981, she and Owen had divorced, and she began to make plans to move to Boston and look for work. The divorce was friendly, and both Janice and Owen assumed legal responsibilities for the boys: Janice was named managing conservator, which made her responsible for choosing their schools, doctors, and other caregivers; and as possessor conservator, Owen was responsible for providing food, clothing, and shelter and arranging their transportation.

❦ When Tony was six, he began living away from home during the academic year as a full-time student at the Texas School for the Blind and Visually Impaired in

Austin. Here, Tony received piano lessons for the first time, in addition to music therapy; and he received instruction in orientation and mobility, communication, motor development, social skills, daily living skills, and physical education. One report from the school provides detailed descriptions of Tony's physical and developmental challenges at this age. In the section on Tony's motor skills at age seven, the report stated:

> *Tony walks maintaining his balance while pushing or pulling a toy or while carrying an object. He walks quickly with a sighted guide, but resists running. . . . Tony does not jump over obstacles, balance on one foot, or hop on one foot. He has an immature throwing pattern with little trunk rotation and poor object release. . . . Although he uses a pincer grasp when instructed to "pinch," he frequently uses immature prehension patterns (four fingers against palm, without opposing use of them). He displays remarkably coordinated use of hands and individual use of fingers when playing the piano and when rhythmically beating a drum. However, a coordinated use of hands is not utilized on some lower level tasks. For example, he attempts to stack blocks using one hand.*

In terms of perceptual abilities, the report indicated that Tony could recognize familiar objects such as a toothbrush and a tricycle, but he could not match objects by shape or size. In addition, Tony could name some of the sounds he heard in his environment, but he often did not respond to them with appropriate actions.

Tony's social development at age seven was described by several observations in the report:

> *Tony prefers playing independently to interacting with adults or peers. . . . Tony does not use an adult as a resource. For example, when he needs assistance to pull his T-shirt down over his head, he says, "uh-oh," but does not call anyone or reach out for help. Tony does not respond appropriately to the presence of peers or to their voices. He will show interest in the same object that a peer is playing with, but he tries to take the object away instead of parallel play. Tony does not initiate appropriate interactions with peers. At times he initiates aggressive interactions.*

> *Tony . . . reacts to frustrating situations by tantrums, self-stimulating (waving his hands in air) and "tuning out" (vocalizing inappropriately, echoing television programs, etc.). . . . Tony does not seek out a favorite object or toy for comfort in a stressful situation. Although he says "please" and "thank you" in appropriate situations, it appears to be a trained response rather than a meaningful social dialog.*

The report also stated that Tony responded attentively to musical stimuli, but his attention span for nonmusical activities was brief—approximately one or two minutes at the most. His self-stimulatory mannerisms included flapping his hands while rhythmically moving his body back and forth, pressing on his eyes, echoing words he heard around him, and turning in circles while flapping his hands at the sides of his head. The teachers also observed that Tony could not button or unbutton his clothes and could not find the sleeve holes in his T-shirts. He could brush his hair by himself, but he often picked up food with his left hand rather than using a spoon and required someone to cut his meat or other hard-to-chew foods for him.

When Tony was home for the summer in 1981, Janice explained to the boys that she was soon going on a trip and that they would stay with Papa until she came to get them. She made all the arrangements for Tony to return to school in Austin and Ralph to attend kindergarten in the fall. With those plans in place, she hooked up a U-Haul trailer to her Chevy Nova hatchback, loaded her furniture and other belongings, and set off for Boston. When she arrived, she moved into an apartment that a Massachusetts friend whom she had met in Texas had already checked out for her.

Janice immediately scheduled a tour of Perkins with

Larry Melander, the principal of Perkins's lower school, with whom she had been talking on the phone for several months. The school was everything she had expected and more: Tours of the leafy, historic campus and meetings with administrators convinced Janice that Tony would thrive there. Her job search was not as productive, however. After all her hard work and a triple major, in education-heavy Boston, all her degree would get her was a minimum-wage job in a daycare center.

During this period, Janice frequently called Owen to talk to Tony and Ralph, and things appeared to be fine. One day in October, however, Janice's call was answered by an older-sounding Hispanic woman who didn't speak English. When Janice asked to speak to Owen, the woman said he wasn't there.

Donde esta? Janice asked.

Pyote.

Janice had no idea what the woman meant; the word sounded like *peyote,* a hallucinogenic plant.

Donde? she asked again.

Pyote—es un lugar en Tejas.

A place in Texas . . . Janice hung up and got out her map. The tiny town lay about 250 miles west of El Paso and one mile from the abandoned Pyote Air Force Station that, during World War II, had affectionately been called Rattlesnake Bomber Base. The town of about four hundred people included ranches spread throughout central Ward County, and Owen had taken a job as a ranch hand, bringing Tony and Ralph along.

Janice was frantic to get back. She loaded all of her things back into a U-Haul trailer and drove to South Dakota to put everything in storage at her parents' house. From there Janice called her sister Linda in Rapid City and asked whether Linda could take time off from work to go with her to Texas to find Tony and Ralph. Linda agreed. She met Janice in Pierre, and the two set off for West Texas.

Finding and recovering the boys turned out to be a fiasco straight out of a B western. Janice and Linda went to the local sheriff, but he explained that if she went out to the ranch and Owen refused to come out and talk, there was nothing anyone could do. Finally, the sheriff put his deputy in charge. The deputy admitted that he knew where Owen was, and he volunteered to show them.

Janice and Linda followed the deputy's car for miles through the dusty plains until they finally got to the gate of the ranch. After going through the gate and closing it behind them, they drove for another ten miles to get to the two houses on the property: a farmhouse and a nearby ranch house. To Janice's relief, the two boys were walking between the two houses with Owen. She quickly got out of the car and walked toward the yard before the deputy had a chance to get out of his car and explain anything to Owen, such as the fact that she didn't have a court order. Owen called out to Janice that she didn't have to get a court order to find him and the kids. "What did you expect me to do when you moved the boys without telling me and I had no idea where you were?" she asked him. She then crouched down and called out to Tony. "Tony, do you want to come to Grandma's house and play the piano?" Tony grinned at the sound of her voice and shouted back, "Yes!" He ran in Janice's direction, and she met him partway, picked him up with a big squeeze, and brought him back to Linda. Then Janice crouched again and spread both arms toward the other boy, saying, "Ralph, do you want to come home to Mama?" He ran to her, too, and they put both boys in the car.

Owen went into the house and returned with an armful of the boys' clothes, which Janice put in the trunk. The deputy watched this interaction and told Janice that because everything seemed okay, he would leave. She got into the car and drove until they were out of the county, stopping at the first motel they could find in order to give the boys a bath.

Janice, Linda, and the boys drove up to Pierre. With

winter coming, Janice decided to stay at her parents' house to regroup. Janice wanted to get Tony and Ralph settled in school as soon as possible, and she needed some time to rethink her career objectives for Boston. With luck, she would be able to get more teaching experience in Pierre.

❧ It was odd being back in the old house, especially in the upstairs apartment section in which Janice and Louie had lived for a time early in their marriage. It was also strange for Janice to deal with her mother as a parent for the first time; their very different philosophies of childrearing clashed from the beginning. Edna believed in the strict, "spare the rod, spoil the child" approach, while Janice felt free to argue that, yes, spoiling the child is good, and she didn't believe in spanking. She knew the effects firsthand and had long ago vowed to never inflict that upon her own children. Janice's father did not get involved in such discussions; he stayed quiet in the background.

In a short time, Janice had the boys enrolled in school. Ralph began spending part of the day in a Head Start program and taking speech therapy sessions provided by the Pierre school district, and Tony attended the South Dakota School for the Visually Handicapped. This school was located in Aberdeen, about 160 miles northeast of Pierre.

Janice drove to and from Aberdeen several times with Tom Sogaard, the Pierre school system's director of special services, to work out Tony's Individualized Education Program (IEP). During those long drives, she talked to Sogaard about the legal issues she had researched in order to understand all of the rights that Tony could claim as a multiply disabled student. Once they got to the meetings, Sogaard referred to these facts in detail as if he had been researching the issues for weeks. Janice was happy to contribute to the process in this way, and Sogaard continued to be dedicated to Tony's educational opportunities throughout the family's stay in South Dakota.

From December 1981 to April 1982, Tony's schedule consisted of ten days at the school in Aberdeen, then home for four days. Janice drove him at first. Her Nova did not have a heater (her father checked it out and discovered that it had never been installed in the factory), so she and Tony would always stop halfway at a café to drink hot chocolate and warm up their numb feet. When Janice learned that these weekday drives prevented her from getting work in the schools, she pursued public transportation for Tony. She had asked Sogaard whether there were any openings in Pierre. He had told her that, although she was qualified, her absences on Mondays and Fridays would prevent continuity in the classroom and lessen her chances of getting hired.

The district offered three types of transportation: mileage reimbursement for the parent's driving; fare for the bus, which was ridiculously slow and seldom chosen; or private air transportation. Janice chose the last option, and Tony began flying to and from Aberdeen with pilot Jeff Ice of Ice Flight Services. State law mandated that the school district could not spend more than $3,000 per year per family for this transportation, so when Tony's cost exceeded that amount, the school had to use their own drivers and cars to get him to and from school.

At the South Dakota School for the Visually Handicapped (now called the South Dakota School for the Blind and Visually Impaired), which was founded in 1900, Tony received instruction in daily living skills such as eating and dressing, training to develop his fine motor skills, individual speech sessions, and group interaction sessions for social development. He also received one hour of music therapy every day. During his free time before lunch, he was allowed to play the piano. The staff installed a buzzer system on the doors of the deaf-blind dormitory where Tony had his room because he had a habit of wandering around at night before falling asleep, but otherwise he made progress at the school. His music therapist, Susan Leonard, noted that "Tony has a very good ear for music and should develop perfect pitch when he acquires the knowledge of notes and keys." All of the staff at the school were well trained and caring, but Janice was anxious to find a setting in which music could become an even stronger element of Tony's training and development. Janice learned that there was also a music therapist at a school for the disabled on the other side of the state. After researching the program, she scheduled Tony to be transferred to the Black Hills Special Services Cooperative in Pluma.

In this program, Tony took special education classes, speech and language therapy, and music therapy. The school also arranged for four one-hour piano lessons each week with Marianne Bieber, a teacher with a private studio in the nearby town of Lead. The program outlined detailed and ambitious goals for Tony's music, such as writing an original song, learning to play at proper tempos, and improving his piano technique. Music was also used as a motivator and reward throughout his day. Tony quickly learned that if he completed a task for his teacher, he would be able to hear some music: Five blocks placed into a can, for example, would earn him thirty seconds of music on the cassette player. This method was remarkably effective. Gradually, Tony focused more clearly on his activities until the musical rewards were no longer necessary; he was content to hear "good job!" and his teacher's applause as a motivator.

The Black Hills program was not a residential setting,

so arrangements were made for Tony to live with "foster parents" the Reverend Albert Peters and his wife, Betty, who lived in the nearby town of Spearfish. Tony went home to Pierre every other weekend for the first few months by car and then by commercial airline. The Peters became Tony's beloved surrogate family, and he remembers them fondly to this day. Tony couldn't wait to get to their house every day to play the two-manual organ they bought just for him, and more than once he got up in the middle of the night to play. The Peters described life with Tony in an edition of the Black Hills Special Services Cooperative newsletter:

It is 3:30 in the morning, and the patriotic sounds of "The Star Spangled Banner" float up the stairs. Our blind, autistic foster child (who is an excellent musician and has his own time schedule) has decided that it is morning. Shortly, the loud demand, "I want to eat!" will follow the sounds of the music. If the call for food doesn't result in immediate attention, the cry "I want a hug!" will join the other sounds.

Now it is decision time. If we respond to the "I want a hug," will we reinforce the early morning waking? . . . How often have you said to a child, "We will get up when it is light?" But this boy lives in the dark at all times. . . .

But support from the Special Services Cooperative is always there. We can call any time of the day or night (and believe us, we have). . . . If the early morning rendition of "The Star Spangled Banner" has upset the routine, you can be assured that the other lovely sounds filling our home at other times are deeply appreciated.

Before she became Tony's private piano teacher as part of the Black Hills program, Marianne Bieber had heard him play at a recital and was astounded by his ability. She had attended a piano recital given by one of the faculty at Black Hills State College, and after the artist left the stage and the audience filed out, Tony went onstage and started playing. Marianne was struck by the distinctive style and beauty of the playing, and she curiously returned to the hall to see what was happening. "It was amazing to hear such a beautiful sound coming out of a young person," she recalled. "It was an exceptional sound that came out of the piano."

When Tony came to Bieber's studio for his first lesson, she was apprehensive about how much he might understand because he did not speak other than to echo what she said, and she had no training in special education. But Bieber had received suggestions from the program's music therapist, Robyn Swanson, and she began to teach him scales so that he could improve his fingering. She guided his hands to play the scale with the correct fingers and spoke the numbers of the fingering as he played (the thumb is 1, index finger is 2, and so on). Fingering involves bringing the thumb underneath to start again after using the third finger, and Bieber counted out "1-2-3, 1-2-3-4-5" as she played the eight notes of a scale. Tony echoed her words, but she discovered that he didn't understand the connection, because he went back to his own technique as soon as she took her hand away. "He said, '1-2-3, 1-2-3-4-5,' but he played 1-2-3-4-5, 4-5-4; his last two fingers simply flew over each other," Bieber said. "For the last three notes, those fingers just fluttered up the rest of the scale. He was very agile at doing that, probably because he had always been doing it that way."

At the end of that first lesson, Bieber sent Tony home with a cassette recording of Prokofiev's *Peter and the Wolf*, a very popular symphonic masterpiece with narration. The thirty-five-minute piece comprises fifteen short sections that tell the story of Peter's adventures. When Tony came to his next lesson after the weekend, he sat down and played the entire piece. His rendition was harmonically complete, as he had reinterpreted all the harmonies of the string, woodwind, and brass sections for the piano. "That was pretty impressive," said Bieber. "He has a brain like a tape recorder."

Together with Swanson, Bieber expanded Tony's repertoire to include all the classical genres—baroque, classical, romantic, and twentieth-century—as well as more jazz, pop, and easy listening pieces. Swanson observed that Tony was remarkably sensitive to the idiosyncrasies of each of these musical styles, had an excellent ear for "tonal recognition," and remembered every piece he learned: "After Tony has thoroughly learned a piece of music, he does not forget it." An interesting detail of this early period of Tony's piano training involves his challenge with a particular form of music. According to Swanson, he had a difficult time with ABA form because he did not want to repeat the A section after playing the B. "He tries, but it is a difficult task for him to accomplish," she wrote. After several listenings, Tony could finally learn the piece accurately, but it took time and patience. He had no problem learning a piece that consisted of only two sections (A and B). Swanson also observed that Tony's left hand was markedly weaker, probably because he was accustomed to simply playing chords with that hand rather than melodies or other musical structures. She suspected that Tony's "innate chordal memory" had forced this habit, and she and Bieber worked diligently on improving his left-hand skill. Swanson and Bieber also observed that Tony much preferred to hear lower pitches than higher ones, and when he sang, he used a much lower voice than that of an eight-year-old child.

Tony's classroom teacher was also aware of his amazingly sensitive hearing. "His hearing is incredible," said Ronda Feterl. "The first day I had him, I took him onto the playground, and he stopped and said, 'A meadowlark is singing.' There were traffic sounds and everything, and I had to really listen for a few moments for that specific sound."

After six months in the Black Hills program, Tony's progress report from Swanson stated that his "attention span has greatly improved, [and] he responds much quicker to new ideas and is eager to demonstrate his abilities." His work with speech and language did not develop as rapidly, however. "Tony's responses are inconsistent from day to day due to his lack of cooperation and tuning out behaviors," reported his speech therapists. They noted that Tony had begun to occasionally interact and converse appropriately with adults because they provided structure and control in the situation, but he was not yet ready to talk to children his own age.

About three months after Janice and her sons arrived in Pierre, Janice found a place for them to live, and they moved out of the Stepaneks' house. Janice also learned about a job training course being offered to recipients of Aid to Families with Dependent Children (AFDC), and she visited the office to apply. The department told Janice that because she already had a college degree, she wasn't qualified for the training; but she explained that she had not been able to find work in her field and needed training in another area. After a team from the Dakota Plains Legal Services argued Janice's case in a meeting, she was allowed to take the course. She learned how to use WordStar, a word processing program, pumped up her typing skills, and was given an introduction to basic accounting. Janice thought it was an excellent strategy for the state to teach young mothers how to use computers so they could get off welfare and into state jobs (the state was the largest employer in South Dakota), and she hoped it would increase her chances of finding work in Boston.

After finishing the course in the spring of 1983, Janice packed another U-Haul trailer, hitched it to her aging Nova hatchback, and headed east. Without realizing it, she was moving home . . . to ancestral home turf, at least. The pioneer roots that her maternal ancestors had stretched to South Dakota originated in eastern Massachusetts, and every mile along the interstate brought Janice and her boys closer to a new life grounded in that determined spirit.

Chapter Five

A NEW VOCABULARY

"Your sound is like, it's like your sweat.
You know, it's your 'sound.' "

—*Miles Davis*

JANICE'S GOAL TO PROVIDE as many musical opportunities as possible for Tony from the beginning, starting with his first organ lessons in El Paso, served her son in many ways through the years. Not only did a music reward system help Tony develop many of his motor and other skills throughout his elementary-school-age years, but playing with extremely talented young musicians in his teens in Massachusetts also had a tremendous impact upon his ability to communicate. As the young pianist's musical vocabulary deepened, he became more comfortable and adept with the language of words.

Bo Winiker, a professional jazz trumpeter with whom

Tony now performs and records in Boston, has witnessed his friend's remarkable transformation as a communicator in both music and language. "After playing together for fifteen years, we're on the same wavelength," Winiker said. "Sometimes I'll play a motif, and Tony will play it back, or harmonize it, or take it a step further. We bounce ideas off each other." Winiker is impressed with many aspects of Tony's musicianship, but one of the most amazing traits that he observes year after year is Tony's extraordinary grasp of so many musical styles. "Tony is in essence a walking encyclopedia of American popular music and jazz," Winiker said. "He has successfully created his own style from every musical experience that he has had. That goes for gospel, rhythm and blues, pop—everything that he's listened to. He has his own unique style in which he sounds like Tony DeBlois; he's gone past the stage of trying to emulate any one musician."

Winiker considers Tony a fellow professional whose sophisticated level of performance places him among the small fraction of those musicians who are great, not just good. This greatness is part of Tony's mysterious and spectacular gifts as a savant; gifts that have been nurtured by many people along the way. The move to Massachusetts introduced Tony to a new set of piano teachers and other dedicated music instructors who helped develop his vocabulary both linguistically and musically.

The Perkins School for the Blind, which sits on thirty-eight acres along the Charles River in Watertown, Massachusetts, began as a small program for blind students held in a Boston home in 1832. In 1833, the school moved into the larger home of Thomas Perkins, a trustee, and was named to honor his generosity. Many famous figures have been affected by the school, including graduate Anne Sullivan and her most famous student, Helen Keller. Keller's mother learned about the school after reading Charles Dickens's book *American Notes,* in which he described the amazing work the school was doing with a deaf-blind girl just like her daughter. Helen entered the school when she was eight years old and spent four years studying with Sullivan, who became her lifelong teacher and friend. By 1912, the school had outgrown its home in the city, and it was moved about nine miles west to Watertown.

Janice had learned a great deal about Perkins's history and curriculum over the years through phone calls with Larry Melander and during her first trip to Boston in 1981. She was impressed by the small classes and especially struck by the way the teachers interacted with the students; they spoke to the children in a more personal, conversational, and adult way than some of the other teachers who had worked with Tony. Janice had been anxious to move to Boston not only for the school but also to put Tony in a more cultured environment where he could be exposed to a high caliber of music and good after-school music programs. She had felt the same way in Texas.

Janice and Ralph moved to Massachusetts in May 1983, while Tony stayed behind in South Dakota to finish his school year in the Black Hills. When the Pierre school system learned that Janice had moved, they informed her that the current school district in Massachusetts was now financially responsible for Tony's last weeks at the Black Hills Cooperative. With legal help from South Dakota, Janice successfully disputed this claim by proving that the financial responsibility belongs to the state in which the student resides. She had hoped to transfer Tony to Perkins directly from Aberdeen, but the state demanded that she try other options in South Dakota before going out of state to find the best school to fit his needs. Although Tony made progress at the Cooperative, Janice felt that a school for the blind would give him the best possible learning environment, and a school in a cultural center such as Boston would also give him many musical opportunities.

Ever since Tony had revealed his remarkable talent as a child back in Texas, Janice had vowed to nurture his musical gift as much as possible so that he could spend the rest of his life doing what he loved. Even though his autism put up many obstacles to the idea of forging a career as a working musician, Janice never ruled it out. She had made the best use of the resources South Dakota had to offer during their stay, and she knew that bigger things awaited them in Massachusetts.

❦ At the end of their cross-country drive in May 1983, Janice and Ralph moved into a small, two-bedroom apartment in Stoneham, an affluent suburb about nine miles north of Boston. The tiny kitchen opened into the dining/living room area, where Janice placed Tony's Kimball organ, a hutch, a couch, and a coffee table. With the addition of the round table in the "dining" area, there was just enough room to walk around the coffee table to get to the hallway or the kitchen. Although she did not yet realize it, living in the greater Boston area put Janice in the region in which her ancestor Benjamin Allbee had lived throughout his life in America. She now lived just eighteen miles from Mendon, the town in which Allbee built his last house and from which he fled Metacom's historic raid.

On her first full day in Stoneham, before she had even unpacked the car, Janice met with Frank Gagliardi, EdD, director of special education for the Stoneham School District, to discuss placements for Tony and Ralph. Then Janice made a call to the governor's Office of Handicapped Affairs for support. Advocate Brad

Pearson assured her that her new school district would provide the best possible opportunities for Tony and Ralph, and he promised to help her every step of the way. From that day, Pearson became a solid ally who was always there to help Janice through the maze of school system bureaucracy and state education laws. Pearson became a friend who could be counted on to bring things back into perspective whenever Janice began to feel a bit overwhelmed raising two adolescent special-needs boys. At one point, when Janice poured out her soul to him about how little money she had to spend on her boys to make them as independent as possible, Pearson said, "Jan, you've given something to Tony and Ralph that no one else could ever give them; you've given them a legacy of love."

Dr. Gagliardi—who ultimately got along very well with Janice, even when they were arguing opposite sides of a dispute regarding Tony's program—also pointed out in their first meeting that Janice's plan to enroll Tony in the Perkins School for the Blind was unrealistic because it was a private school, not part of the public school system. Janice had to admit that she had no idea that private schools for the blind even existed, because all the schools she had dealt with thus far had been state run. But, fortunately, this point was just another false alarm. When the district received all of Tony's documentation and learned exactly what his needs were, they agreed to place him at Perkins. Nine-year-old Tony's first days on campus were in June 1983, for an evaluation in which administrators determined which classes he would take, which level of the lower school he would enter (students usually entered the upper school in their early teens), and other details of his placement.

From those first days of his evaluation period, Tony fell in love with the school. Although Perkins had begun to enroll children with multiple disabilities after the handicapped legislation of 1974, many of the students did not have any disabilities other than blindness or impaired vision, which created a very different atmosphere than the Black Hills Cooperative. That school had been set up exclusively for extremely disabled children with cerebral palsy and other physical and behavioral problems, and their resources were stretched to deal with blindness on top of those other disabilities. This fact, in addition to the mature way in which the teachers at Perkins communicated with the students, gave Janice hope that Tony's language skills would improve there more than they had anywhere else. Janice had hoped that Tony could live at the school for at least the first year so that he would have more access to living skills and other training, but he was not eligible for residential placement because his previous setting in South Dakota had not been residential. Special education law states that a child cannot move into a more restrictive environment, so residential placement was not an option. It was great to have Tony at home, however, even if he was missing out on some of the socialization opportunities that living at Perkins would provide.

The school began to develop a curriculum for Tony that included programs in social skills, language, arts and crafts, physical education, mobility, and music—each tailored to his specific needs. One of the objectives set down by his daily living skills instructor, for example, addressed how easily Tony became distracted when eating, either by his own thoughts or by hearing other students' voices. Tony's instructors would work to remind him to use his utensils properly, not pick up food with his hands, engage in back-and-forth conversation at the table rather than constantly asking questions, and lower the volume of his voice in a restaurant.

In Tony's first year at Perkins, some of his activities of daily living (ADL) skills became an issue, primarily the ability to teach him very basic tasks such as bathing. Perkins administrators told Janice that this training wasn't appropriate for a day placement student, and they asked her to find an alternative. She made a case with the Stoneham school system that as a certified special education instructor, she herself was legally and professionally qualified to provide this training. The school system agreed to hire Janice as Tony's ADL instructor, and she submitted an official educational plan that she and Tony would follow for the rest of that school year. In addition to learning how to take a bath, Tony worked with his mom on peeling fruit, opening up packages of food, and dealing with packs of plastic utensils that he would use on school outings, picnics, and airplane trips. After the first year, Tony was allowed to stay overnight at the school one night a week for language development with his peers and to learn how to make a bed, pack a suitcase, and other living skills. Janice felt that these abilities were important aspects of Tony's vocational training because as a working musician he would one day travel to gigs and need to know how to deal with life on the road.

⤝ By September of that first autumn in Massachusetts, Tony was settled in at Perkins, but Ralph had only begun what would become a long, complex string of placements in special ed settings. Unconvinced that Ralph needed special education, the school district initially placed him in a regular first-grade classroom, but he lasted only six weeks in that setting. At age seven, Ralph had already begun lying, stealing, and acting out other behavioral problems that would not only shift him into different schools but also bring Janice into court from time to time. Two of Ralph's transfers were the result of the entire special ed program shutting down, but he was also taken out of schools for problems that the facilities just weren't able to handle. Janice tried to make progress with Ralph on one of these problems—with inconsistent results.

Janice's Journal

Ralph had fire-setting problems when we were in Stoneham, so I decided to teach fire safety to him myself and arranged a reward system for having a fire-safe week. In the winter, the reward was a candlelight supper at home, where Ralph got to light the candles. In the summertime, we went out to Harold Parker State Forest, and I taught him how to make a safe fire for a hot-dog roast. His summer rewards were helping me tend to the campfire. I told Ralph that under the worst circumstances, if he was lost outside and freezing cold, he could light a fire in an empty, enclosed metal container. A little later, when Ralph ran away from home (for the first time), it was cold, and he followed my instructions by crunching up the Yellow Pages book he found in a phone booth, lighting it, and throwing it into a metal container. When the police brought Ralph home, he shouted, "But Mom, I knocked on the green box and it was full, so I knocked on the blue box and it was empty—I put the fire in the blue box!" Unfortunately, the blue box was *a US Postal Service mailbox. The judge slammed him with a $50,000 bail bond, then changed his mind the next day and put Ralph on probation. He was eleven years old.*

Ralph ran away from home often; in one particularly tough year, he ran away sixty times. "I used every ounce of my private detective experience in dealing with Ralph," Janice said. Two years after the mailbox incident, Ralph came home with another problem that he would repeat in years to come. Janice describes Ralph as a very helpful person, and when he met a teenager on the street one day who was having car problems, he offered to help. After they started the car, the teenager told Ralph he could actually take it for a drive because it was his mom's car, and he wasn't supposed to have it; he wanted to get it off his hands. Ralph drove the car home and parked it in front of the house, and a few hours later, the police came and identified it as a stolen vehicle. The teenager had hot-wired the car right in front of Ralph and easily convinced him to drive away with it.

❦ Unlike Janice's work with Ralph, her special efforts with Tony usually centered around his musical training. When Janice learned that the piano lessons Tony received at Perkins focused entirely on classical music, she looked for a jazz teacher in the area who could give him private lessons at home. She found an ad in the paper for lessons by local jazz pianist Ron Merullo, who described himself as a blues teacher, and she hired him to teach Tony once a week. After settling in for a few months, she learned about another teacher, Janis Colburn, who taught in Pelham, New Hampshire, about an hour's drive away from Stoneham. Colburn could work with Tony on a variety of styles on both piano and organ, and she also utilized the cutting-edge technology of a Passport Designs music synthesizer driven by an Apple II computer that "spoke" to the player. Janice signed Tony up for weekly lessons. Within weeks, Colburn arranged for Tony to be the guest organist for a service at Pleasant Street Methodist Church in Salem, Massachusetts, where she was the organist and choir director.

From the start, Janice wanted Tony to share his talent with the community with appearances such as the one in Salem. Prior to that event, he had played his first "professional" gig at the Sunshine Nursing Home in Stoneham, for which he had received a fee of thirty-five dollars. His next appearances were in July 1983, with programs at the Stoneham Senior Citizens Center and Stoneham Public Library. These performances launched what Janice came to call Tony's career on the "senior citizen/nursing home circuit," in which he played for fees of fifty dollars an hour.

One of Tony's grade-school-age performances resulted in an unexpected return. Tony had joined a Cub Scouts troop in Stoneham, and he attended meetings once a month and worked on activities at home with Janice. When his troop was asked to sing a patriotic song at the Distinguished Citizen Award ceremony for Frank Bretton, former president of Marshalls stores, Tony played a couple of piano solos at the event. Among the hundreds of attendees that night was Marc Cabot, owner of Cabot Hosiery Mills in Vermont. A self-described classical and jazz piano aficionado, Cabot was so moved by Tony's playing that he offered him a special gift. "Tony played marvelous music," he said, "and I had the perfect opportunity to do a mitzvah, to do something for somebody in need." When he learned that Tony didn't have a piano at home, he decided to give him the rarely used one in his Riverside, New York, apartment. Cabot had no idea how to get the piano from the sixth-floor apartment to Tony's house in Massachusetts, however. Another man at his table suggested that he turn around and talk to an executive sitting behind him who operated a fleet of trucks, including deliveries for Marshalls stores. When Cabot told him about the piano, the executive offered to pick it up the following week and deliver it to Tony's house. After the dinner, Cabot met Tony and said, "Tony, you have a piano." Tony said, "No, I have a Kimball Swinger." Cabot said, "Now you have a piano, too." The piano was delivered the following week, as promised, and Cabot kept in touch with the family. "I got several nice letters from Janice over the years letting us know of Tony's progress," he said.

"Imagine my surprise when this piano turned out to be a two-year-old Baldwin valued at three thousand dollars," said Janice. To this day, the Baldwin upright is the only piano that Tony has ever owned.

Tony's piano teacher at Perkins, Adele Trytko, had been teaching for several years at Perkins and was very familiar with the "special organization" that each blind pianist has at the keyboard. During Tony's weekly lessons, she would play along with him so that he would have the piece in his ear, and, like Tony's other teachers, she worked on his fingering, which was essential in classical pieces. "Sometimes, when blind students play a lot on their own, they develop their own patterns of fingering," she said, "which is however they feel comfortable in reaching different notes."

Trytko saw tremendous potential in Tony and found that he could memorize complex classical pieces as quickly as simpler popular music. While learning Beethoven's Sonata, op. 2, no. 1, for example, almost all the notes were there a short time after Tony first listened to the piece on the cassette she gave him to listen to at home. Perfecting the piece, making sure that Tony played every note, took repetition during his lessons, but he learned the entire piece and performed the first movement, Allegro, in his first solo recital at the school in 1986, at age twelve. Other pieces on that first Perkins recital included Chopin's Mazurka in F, op. 68, no. 3; Prelude in D-flat, op. 28, no. 15; and Prelude in G, op. 28; six movements from Schumann's *Kinderszenen* (Scenes from Childhood), op. 15; the Vivo e delicato movement from Prokofiev's Prelude in C., op. 12, no. 7; and the Allegro movement from Mozart's Sonata in C, K. V. 545.

Every year, Trytko challenged Tony with more advanced repertoire, including virtuosic pieces such as Beethoven's Sonata no. 8, "Pathetique," which he performed in a solo recital in his last year at the school.

Tony's lower-school classroom teacher, Storm Barkus, found creative ways to utilize Tony's love of music to help develop his language. A pianist herself, Barkus enjoyed bringing music into the classroom as well as into other activities. One of the games Tony enjoyed the most involved making up songs to describe what he was doing. Barkus described some of her work with Tony, including this game:

> *When I first met Tony, he would imitate language; you would say, "It's hot today," and he'd say, "It's hot today." Echolalic language was part of his autistic responses. In order to break out of that, we'd have spontaneous activities such as playing ball or tug-of-war to have more spontaneous and more meaningful language development coming from that. Because of Tony's musical ability, when we did the washing in one of the cottages, we'd sing in operatic voices about how we were carrying the wash and folding it and putting it away. That became a game that was really fun for Tony.*

Between Janice's regular meetings to develop and review her boys' Individual Education Programs (IEPs); meetings with physical and occupational therapists, school administrators, social security officers, and Ralph's probation officer; and driving Tony to his lessons and other activities, Janice found time to work as a temporary secretary. The only people she met outside the office were teachers and therapists, and she had very little time or interest in socializing. In June 1987, however, she got a call from one of Tony's educational aides at Perkins, a musician named Tom DeBlois, who wanted to take Tony home with him for the weekend. He had told Tony all about the two-manual Kawai organ he had in his house, on which he practiced for his job as a church organist and choir director. Tony, then thirteen years old, was eager to check it out. Janice said she'd consider it, but she wanted to meet Tom first and draw up some papers for him to sign so that he would assume responsibility for Tony's safety during the visit.

At that first meeting, Janice was surprised to find herself engrossed in a conversation about how Perkins nurtured Tony's music, the struggles of raising two special-needs sons, the role of music in education and child development, and life in general. Tom was sixteen years younger than she, but he was obviously very interested in her story and enjoyed talking . . . and talking and talking. It was one of those meetings in which two people realize that they click, and part of Janice's attraction also came from seeing Tom's caring commitment to Tony. Janice agreed to let Tom take Tony for the weekend—after he signed the papers—and Tom DeBlois officially entered her life.

During that first conversation, Tom also reminded Janice that she had already met him about a year earlier at one of Tony's IEP meetings. Tom vividly recalled that Janice had questioned his approach to some aspect of

Tony's care and told him, "This is how I do it at home, and I think it will work better." Tom thought that this woman had some nerve telling him how to do his job.

Tom and Janice had many more talks, and Tom helped out by driving them to Tony's lessons, to camp, to the airport—all of which gave him more opportunities to be with Janice. Tom, a handsome guy with shoulder-length, curly black hair and a thick moustache, had worked at his hometown church in New Hampshire as the organist and choir director since he was seventeen and attended college as a music major for a couple of years. As a musician, he was not only amazed by Tony's talent but also intrigued by every aspect of savant syndrome. This always gave the couple plenty to talk about, and in the fall of 1987, they had their first official date when Tom asked Janice to a Perkins staff party.

A few months after they started dating, during a dinner dance evening at the Kiwanis Club, Tom asked Janice to marry him. Although they had talked about the age difference, Tom insisted it wasn't a problem, and, even more important, he loved Tony and Ralph and wanted to adopt them and make them all a family. They made plans for a wedding the following summer and, in the meantime, rented a house together in Waltham, just three miles from Tony's school in Watertown.

On June 18, 1988, Tom and Janice were married at

the Little Harbor Chapel in the oceanside town of Portsmouth, New Hampshire. Janice's parents and sister Linda came from South Dakota, Tony played the organ, and Ralph sat up front with them on the bride's side of the aisle. As the ring bearer, Ralph was a bit distracting as he twirled his mom's wedding band on his raised finger throughout much of the ceremony.

After the wedding, Tom signed adoption papers and the boys changed their names. "Ralph had been going around on some of his younger escapades calling himself José," said Janice, "so I said, 'Now's your chance. If you want to change your name, go ahead.'" Both boys replaced remnants of their biological father's name with parts of Tom's name: Ralph Raymond Mooney became Raymond Joseph DeBlois and Anthony Owen Mooney became Anthony Thomas DeBlois. From that time Ralph became known as Ray, and the transition was made easier by the fact that he enrolled in a new school just after the name change, so he got used to the idea in that new setting. A short time after the wedding, another change came to the family with the purchase of a new house in Waltham, about five doors down from the home they had been renting.

At about the same time that the family moved to the new house in Waltham, Tony began taking part in the after-school music program at the Music School at Rivers in Weston, four miles down the road from Waltham. The school was on the campus of the Rivers School, a private college preparatory school for grades six through twelve, and it was housed in a sumptuous New England mansion. Unlike the prep school, the music school was a nonprofit community conservatory that was open to everyone. Janice had been looking for a program in which Tony could play in ensembles to help him socialize with other students through his music. She had scoped out some of the larger programs in the hope that they might have scholarship opportunities. One of her prospects was the after-school program at the New England Conservatory in downtown Boston. Although NEC had a wonderful reputation for its curriculum for younger students, the administrators felt that their class sizes were too big to accommodate Tony. It would be impossible for them to give him the smaller classes and more individualized attention that he needed, so they recommended that Janice contact the Music School at Rivers.

Rivers was a perfect fit, from its small classes to its excellent teachers and great opportunities for Tony to work with other players in jazz ensembles. Janice believed that Tony would be eligible to include the program as part of his entire educational program covered by the school district; but to get him started right away, she paid for the first semester's tuition herself in the summer of 1987. Janice began preparing her case for this program to be considered a viable part of Tony's special-needs education and in 1988 engaged in a hearing with the Waltham school system to make it happen. The case, *Janice Mooney As She Is the Parent of Anthony Mooney v. Waltham School Committee*, BSEA No. 88-1003, considered whether the activities at Rivers constituted a viable part of the educational requirements as outlined in Tony's IEP. Janice argued that ensembles were an integral part of Tony's social and language development, and all parties ultimately agreed. Beginning in 1988, Tony's tuition at Rivers was covered by the Waltham school system.

At Rivers, Tony began studying jazz piano with Paul Barringer, the director of the jazz program. Barringer's first impression of Tony was a mixture of surprise and awe.

> *I had never taught an autistic child before. Usually, the idea of an autistic kid means, to me, antisocial or asocial, nonfunctioning; they don't relate to people; you can't just go up and talk to them. Tony was interesting because he was, from the first, very sociable and very interested, asking, "Who are you?" I was trying to teach certain materials or go over certain musical*

things, and I was constantly being interrupted with his questions. "What do you do?" "Do you like the red line?" He was fascinated with the Boston subway system. He had really good ear-to-hand connection— very good, very strong. And he was able pretty much, so far as we could tell, to play whatever he heard. He could literally play back any chord; I could play the strangest combination of sounds; he could find it immediately and play it back, no problem.

In those first lessons, Barringer also learned some of the commands that Janice used with Tony. She sat in on the first couple of lessons. When Tony interrupted Barringer by playing while he was talking, for example, she would say, "Hands down." Tony obeyed, but she would have to repeat this command throughout the lesson, as would Barringer from time to time in the first couple of years. Tony was so happy to be at these lessons that he behaved quite well overall, and Barringer was surprised to find that their communication "became pretty good, pretty easy in a short time."

Jazz was particularly suited to Tony because it is largely an aural-based tradition in which students learn in the "call and response" method. Instead of reading the music on the page, which many young jazz students cannot do anyway because they've always played by ear, the student learns by listening. The teacher plays part of a melody, the student plays it back, then they move on to the next part and repeat the process until the melody is learned. Once that is done, they move on to the harmonies of the piece that are played primarily with the left hand.

For someone like Tony, this was the ultimate way of learning. He picked up everything immediately, including all the harmonizations to the melodies. "He absorbed the language of jazz improvisation that all jazz musicians know, which we call vocabulary," said Barringer. "That includes rhythmic, melodic, harmonic, and structural elements." A major element of jazz vocabulary is the unique language of jazz masters that performers infuse into their improvisations. To the trained ear, a good jazz performance incorporates familiar phrases that identify specific masters, prompting the listener to recognize a taste of Thelonious Monk, perhaps, or Art Tatum or whomever the performer is moved to echo at that particular moment. Over the years, Barringer gave Tony many recordings of the masters to help him absorb the vocabulary of jazz. As a result, Tony began to use the vocabulary of various artists in his own improvisations.

According to Barringer, Tony was particularly drawn to the style of Chick Corea. He learned a Corea piece entitled "Thunder," which Barringer described as calling for "very advanced, high-level, sophisticated piano playing." Tony's approach to this piece revealed that he was learning to comprehend some of the concepts of jazz completely through the music itself rather than talking about them. "In this song, which is kind of a modal, more open-ended kind of piece, he really got to explore different stuff," said Barringer. "He actually absorbed some of Chick Corea's vocabulary, his way of approaching chords and playing melodies and so on."

Barringer discovered, just as Tony's teacher Marianne Bieber in South Dakota had observed, that Tony had his own approach to piano technique that he had developed from an early age. Barringer often wondered about Tony's concept of the keyboard, which did not appear to be the same as other students he'd worked with. Because Tony was blind, Barringer figured, he did not think in terms of black and white keys; and his fingering technique revealed that he did not think in terms of the two and three patterns of the keys, either. "He's probably feeling some of that," Barringer said, "but it's more like whatever finger happens to be there. He developed a way of sort of sliding into the keys." Tony did make progress in his scales, however, which Barringer returned to again and again to help develop his technique. "He got a handle on that," Barringer said, "but when it came to playing involved melodic passages, different kinds of situations where you had to really change fingers a lot, a lot of thumb crossing, that was very difficult." Tony had his own way of getting around difficult passages, and he reverted to this self-styled approach rather than absorbing a more traditional fingering technique.

Another issue that former teachers had identified as a challenge was Tony's understanding of some musical forms and structures. Once Tony got into jazz ensemble at Rivers—he was immediately placed in the highest level group—he had to be coached for a time on the pattern of returning to the A section of a piece after playing the B section. "I would tell the group, 'Okay, we're going to do the A section this way and the B section this way, and when we get back to A at the end, we're going to close this way,' " said Barringer. "When we were talking about it, Tony wouldn't necessarily get it, but then we'd play, and sometimes I'd have to sit in and direct him a little, and he could do it. So we just had to be a little bit patient in that regard." Tony apparently picked up other clues that helped him play within the correct structure. "He hears musical cues coming up," said Barringer, "and remembers, for example, that when someone gets softer that means that someone else is going to come in. He did really well with that. He's feeling the form structure."

Barringer encountered some mysterious learning

experiences with Tony that to this day he cannot explain. For example, when he's performing, Barringer has a habit of tilting his head slightly to the side so that he's not facing the keyboard. Many of his students pick up this mannerism, too, but he was astonished to see Tony do it. How could a blind person possibly know the position of his teacher's head when he's playing the piano? Another odd situation involved the cassette tapes he gave Tony to listen to at home. Tony couldn't read the labels, of course, but he could identify the tapes by putting them next to one ear and shaking them. Barringer realized that the sixty-minute tapes probably felt lighter than the ninety-minute tapes, but he could not understand the other characteristics of the tapes that made each one so unique to Tony.

Tony's fellow students at Rivers responded to him well; they quickly looked beyond his blindness and autism and simply admired him as a fantastic musician. Said Barringer, "Someone was always there to bring him up to the stage and take him back. They were astounded that here's a blind person who understands chord structure better than anyone and is an amazing soloist. I think he inspired them because they first of all thought, 'How can he do this?'; second, 'Where did he come up with some of these ideas?'; and third, 'Where is he going in the piece now?' Just playing with him was exciting."

One of those fellow students, a seventeen-year-old pianist named Brian Hyett, wrote a moving essay about the impact that Tony had on his music and his life. This essay, reprinted with Brian's permission, offers a teenager's first-person view of Tony's effect on the students around him.

Tony walked to the piano slowly, gracefully, holding his teacher's hand. He felt for the cushion on the bench and then sat on it. I noticed how long his fingers were, and how awkward he looked in his sport coat and tie, which seemed too small. He played the melody of Sonny Rollins's "Ole" very fast. Then, he started to rock back and forth, humming the solo while playing jazz chords with his left hand. Now his teacher approached the piano and said: "Play, Tony, play and don't sing," and Tony began to play the notes with his right hand as beautifully as he sang them. I did not imagine then that this boy, blind and autistic, would change my music. It was at that spring concert at the music school that I decided to study jazz; in the fall, I began.

Now I have found a way to bring from deep within me feelings that I express on the piano. The summer after I began my jazz studies, I played in an ensemble for the first time—drums, an electric bass, two horns, and Tony at the second piano. Of the five members in the group, I learned the most from Tony.

He often danced with his torso like Ray Charles. He sometimes stopped playing altogether to clap for a few seconds before returning to the instrument. Tony struck every note with delicacy. It seemed to me that the keys of the piano found his fingers, and not the other way around. I was frustrated that summer, for I wanted to play as well as Tony and with his ease. My teacher explained how Tony's disabilities affected his music. Mr. Barringer said that Tony was not always aware of what he played or how it sounded to others' ears. I had trouble understanding this. How could someone who played so well not know exactly what he was doing? I was told to pay careful attention to Tony; I could learn a lot by listening to his music. I already had.

Tony's subtle and light touch was something I dreamed of achieving. I worked on bringing into the music whatever mood I was in when I sat down to play. Tony, in a good mood or bad, shaped his music around himself. If he wasn't listening well one day, his playing might be scattered. If he was sharp and attentive, his music had a clear direction. Watching him, I studied myself. His music seemed dependent on his concentration, and so I learned to concentrate.

I have begun to understand Tony better from studying with him in theory class and playing together in jazz concerts month after month. He often plays wildly, skimming over several notes without producing a clear musical idea. Then, in the same sitting, he will play so beautifully that I am longing for more when he is through. Tony DeBlois has taught me more than music. One can't overlook his swaying arms, his large head, eyes opened halfway so they appear functional. But beneath his disabilities is his ability to speak clearly, and listen, and learn. He has worked through his limitations to excel at what he loves. I value his struggle. Unfortunately, Tony cannot comprehend what he has done for me. Through his blindness I am learning of my own. Often, I'm surprised by the music I create that is not written in notes on the page. In Tony's autism, I recognize what I don't understand in myself. I get closer to unraveling this mystery whenever I play.

In 1988, Tony's jazz ensemble at Rivers participated in the Berklee College of Music High School Jazz Festival, where he earned an Outstanding Musicianship Award for his performance with the group. The next year, the ensemble performed in the festival again. In addition to the musicianship award, Tony received a five-hundred-dollar scholarship to Berklee's Summer Performance Program. Janice was thrilled about Berklee's recognition of Tony's talent, but the scholarship only covered a portion of the thirty-five-hundred-dollar cost of the five-week program and the private assistant Tony required. As Janice had done many times before, she gathered her notes together and prepared to request that the summer program be covered by the school district as part of Tony's educational plan. To initiate this process, she sent a letter to Waltham Public Schools rejecting his current IEP, which put the hearing process into motion. She hired the Boston law firm of Bernstein and Bronstein to work on the case, *Anthony DeBlois v. Waltham Public Schools*, BSEA No. 89-1764, which was put before the Massachusetts Department of Education's Bureau of Special Education Appeals.

Among the points that Janice outlined for her attorneys was the fact that it was not significantly more expensive to integrate Tony into a regular program. She wrote up a cost comparison to show that attending the Berklee program and the Rivers school cost only $198.28 more than attending the Perkins and Rivers programs in the summer. "This showed that the cost to integrate Tony into classes and ensembles with regular students was very small, while it also took him into the least restrictive environment," said Janice.

The hearing would take some time. As the Berklee

program was about to start that summer, Janice borrowed on her IRA, borrowed some money from a friend,
and paid the tuition herself.

The school district argued that Tony already received
an education that assured "his maximum possible development in the least restrictive environment," as granted
him by Massachusetts law. His comprehensive program
at Perkins and his after-school music studies at the Rivers
School of Music were sufficient in addressing his special
needs as well as his extraordinary musical talent, they
believed. In his statement used in the case, Dr. Treffert
countered that argument by emphasizing the benefits of
an additional program like the Berklee summer session.

*It is my opinion that whatever can be done to further
the musical exposure, education, and advantage of
Anthony DeBlois is not merely a fascination with his
astonishing talent but rather a direct investment in
furthering his overall development to allow him to
reach his full potential and become as self-reliant and
self-supporting an individual as possible in the least
restrictive alternative living circumstance available to
him. Increasing his exposure to music and other musicians, such as would be accomplished at the Special
Summer Performance Program, is far more than a
"cultural experience" but indeed is an extension of his*

special education experience to give him full advantage of using his very special skills to offset his otherwise very impeding handicap. I highly recommend this summer performance experience as the best investment of these summer months for him toward a full educational objective as an integral part of the best special education experience that can be provided him.

Paul Barringer also participated in the hearing, and in a written statement, he highlighted the fact that Tony's musical educational experiences were preparing him for a vocation in music.

Tony is already well equipped to play as a freelance solo pianist for various situations. Based on his skills and his very high musical aptitude, he will definitely be ready to perform as a mature, professional musician in five years, both as a soloist and as a member of a group. With his unique combination of talents, Tony will have many outlets as a pianist. Given the right exposure and support, he will be very capable of sustaining himself as a performer.

Tony's creative and musical gifts give him the ability to be uniquely individual as an improviser and to create pieces of unusual beauty and depth. Any

problems he has as an autistic person never get in his
way while he is performing.

Tony has much to contribute to the world of music,
and I strongly urge anyone who can to help give him
this chance to fully develop his musical artistry.

Additional testimony came from Storm Barkus, one of Tony's classroom teachers at the Perkins School for the Blind, who stated that some of the goals in Tony's IEP would be advanced by his attendance in the Berklee program. Steven Lipman, Berklee's director of admissions, testified that Tony had the potential for a performing career and that the full extent of his talent was as yet unknown. Lipman added that this potential could best be determined by giving Tony the opportunity to play with musicians at his skill level or higher, such as he would encounter in the Berklee summer program.

Everyone involved in the case gathered for hearing sessions in June and July of 1989, and in October, the hearing officer, Reece Erlichman, handed down her decision. She found that the Berklee summer program was a valid addition to Tony's overall special education program, and she ordered that Waltham Public Schools reimburse Janice for the tuition, transportation, and personal aide costs that she had paid for.

This decision validated Janice's argument that Berklee

added an important vocational element to Tony's IEP, and advocates for the handicapped viewed the case as a "landmark step in broadening the definition of special education" that "helps establish music as a vocational skill." Janice's attorney, Eileen Ordover, believed that the decision helped support some of the broad issues about special education. "What is important here is the way the decision focuses attention on the extent to which individual needs, no matter how unique they are, have to be addressed through special education programs," she said.

Tony's involvement in the Berklee Summer Performance Program was a turning point in his life. His mother had long known that he had the potential to become a working musician, and the strides he made in those five weeks proved that playing with excellent musicians and playing in high-level ensembles brought out his best both musically and emotionally. The testimony of Dr. Treffert, Barringer, and others at the hearing confirmed that the experts saw the same potential; and Tony entered a new phase in his personal and professional development.

❧ Since moving to Massachusetts in 1983, Janice had been reading about the link between miscarriages and birth defects and the father's exposure to Agent Orange during active duty in Vietnam. Theories were sprouting up that some men who had been exposed to the herbicide had fertility problems. Agent Orange was the powerful weed-killing compound used by US troops to clear vegetation, destroying enemy cover. It contained dioxin, also known as TCDD, which is the one of the most toxic man-made chemicals on the planet, second only to radioactive waste. Between 1961 and 1971, 21 million gallons of Agent Orange and other herbicides were sprayed in Vietnam, which destroyed 5 million acres of forests and affected up to 2.6 million American military personnel. Although Janice's ex-husband Owen refused to talk about details of his Vietnam experience, she believed that he was exposed to the chemical because of the frontline position he had held in military intelligence.

Janice's Journal

The interpreters are always some of the first people to go in. When they start clearing the area, they start capturing the people, and then intelligence starts interrogating them. My belief is that the sperm of the guys who were around Agent Orange was affected because at the time, from what I have read, there was an increase in hydatidiform pregnancies in Vietnamese women (in these rare "molar" pregnancies, tissue other than an embryo grows in the uterus after fertilization).

Women reported either having miscarriages in the

first six weeks or having stillbirths in the fifth month of the pregnancy, having babies born with clubbing of the hands and feet and liver problems. The things that were happening to me were the types of problems that several people were reporting. Also, with every pregnancy, I carried the baby to longer term; it seemed as if the effects were waning over time.

A lawsuit filed on behalf of Vietnam veterans against the wartime manufacturers of Agent Orange—Dow Chemical, Monsanto, Uniroyal, Diamond Shamrock, et al.—resulted in a settlement in 1984 that awarded financial compensation to more than 200,000 veterans. Studies on the effects of Agent Orange on the troops began in the 1970s and started to be published in the 1980s. As a result, the Veterans Health Administration currently recognizes several diseases, primarily cancers, as associated with exposure to the compound. These include prostate cancer, lung cancer, soft-tissue sarcoma (malignant tumor of the muscle or connective tissue), chronic lymphocytic leukemia, Hodgkin's disease, non-Hodgkin's lymphoma, bronchus and larynx cancer, and others. Agent Orange has also been found to cause type 2 diabetes.

Many of the studies about the effect of Agent Orange on birth defects have been controversial, but statistically

significant relationships have been found. To date, however, the Veterans Administration only recognizes spina
bifida as a birth defect related to Agent Orange. Spina
bifida causes part of the spinal cord to push through an
opening in the spinal column, resulting in paralysis.

The most controversial study of birth defects and
Agent Orange is the ongoing US Air Force Ranch Hand
Study, which studies the veterans who were responsible
for handling the Agent Orange barrels and spraying the
chemical. The study was named after Operation Ranch
Hand, the military's title for herbicide spraying in Vietnam. One of the flaws of the study, critics feel, has been
the subjects themselves; a more realistic group to study
would be the troops on the ground who were exposed
to the spraying. Although the data showed that the
Ranch Hand veterans had twice as many cancers as the
comparison group, the language of the first report in
1984 was altered to lessen the impact of the findings.

The second Ranch Hand study report, published in
1988, was much more forthcoming about the chemical's
link to birth defects. The study analyzed the health of
children born before and after the Vietnam experience.
Prior to Vietnam, the Agent Orange–exposed group had
borne 85 percent as many children with birth defects as
the nonexposed group; after Vietnam, the exposed
group bore 139 percent as many children with birth

defects. The first air force study had said that birth defects among dioxin-exposed families were limited to minor skin lesions, but the second report reversed that conclusion. This study found 80 children born with defects out of 917 total births in the exposed group, versus 48 children born with defects out of 744 total births in the nonexposed group.

Janice's suspicion about Owen's exposure to Agent Orange as a cause of another problem, her miscarriages, is also supported by several studies. The 1988 Ranch Hand report found a direct relationship between the amount of exposure veterans had to dioxin and the frequency of miscarriage. The higher the exposure, the greater the occurrence of miscarriages. Other studies that confirm this link include a report about accidental exposure to dioxin in 1976 in Seveso, Italy, which resulted in a higher rate of miscarriages among those who were exposed.

❧ At about the same time that Tony participated in his first Berklee summer program, he met up with a jazz combo that opened new doors for him. This group continues to be a vital part of his musical development. One day that summer, he ran into the kitchen and shouted, "Jazz brunch! Jazz brunch!" Janice had no idea what he was talking about, but Tony was insistent. "Radio jazz brunch!" he said. She went into his room to hear what he had been listening to, and she realized that he must have heard an advertisement on WERS-FM, the jazz radio station broadcast from Boston's Emerson College. She called up the station and asked whether they had just mentioned a jazz brunch, and the receptionist told her that, yes, they ran an ad about the Winiker Jazz Quartet playing on Sunday at Skipjack's restaurant in downtown Boston. Janice called the restaurant and made a reservation.

The Winiker Jazz Quartet was founded by drummer Bill Winiker and his brother, trumpeter Bo Winiker. At that Sunday's performance, Bill was quietly whistling a harmony part to Bo's solo on the flügelhorn during a piece in the first set. Tony and Janice were sitting at a table right next to the stage area, and Tony began whistling a third line of harmony to accompany Bill's tune. Bill was intrigued by the creativity of that harmonization, and he looked around to see who was doing it. "When the set was over, I went over to their table and introduced myself," said Bill. "Janice introduced Tony and said that her son was a jazz pianist. I told him, 'You sure do great harmonizing,' and he smiled, but he didn't say much." Bill chatted with Janice awhile longer, then turned to Tony again and asked him if he would like to join them for a song or two in the next set. That brought on a big smile, and when the break was over, Janice led Tony to the stage and to the chair in front of the Roland keyboard. Once everyone was in place, Tony took over by calling out the name of a piece by Horace Silver. "He shouted out, 'Nica's Dream!' " said Bill, "which made me laugh and look over at our bass player, Tom Petrakis. I didn't think Tony could play it; it's a complicated piece. But we started out and not only could he play it, he played it so beautifully that I started to tear up."

Tony played with the quartet for the next hour, and the Winikers invited him to come back the following month. Since then, Tony has been heard at Skipjack's with the Winikers once a month. The highlight of his performances at Skipjack's thus far occurred in April 2005, when an entire Boston church choir showed up for brunch after services. Tony had a special guest that day from Maine, a visiting singer friend who took the stage to sing a couple of gospel songs. When the choir group, which was comprised of about forty-five women and five men, came in from the other room to see who was singing so beautifully, one of its members asked if she could sing a couple of songs with the quartet. When this singer burst into her second number, "When the Saints Go Marching In," the entire group began to clap and parade through the room. "It was the most incredible thing that's ever happened at Skipjack's," said Bo. "The rafters were shaking, and I thought the foundation was going to raise up off the ground!" He attributed the excitement to Tony's brilliant accompaniment. "Tony accompanied her so magnificently; nobody in the world could have accompanied this woman as well as Tony did," he said. "That's part of the genius of Tony DeBlois, the fact that he can play great jazz or classical music or gospel. In the split second that the woman started singing, Tony knew what key she was in, and he created something so special. I don't think anyone who was at Skipjack's that day will ever forget it."

The Winikers have nurtured Tony's jazz performance career by recording three CDs with him, each of which has been financed by Janice. The first, *Beyond Words* (2002), is a collection of instrumental standards such as "Body and Soul," "My Funny Valentine," and "I Got Rhythm," in addition to an original piece by Tony entitled "Tony's Blues." Janice came up with the title as a reflection of Tony's lack of conversational speech as well as of the beauty of the playing. The next recording, *Mercer, Mercy Me* (2003), contains fifteen songs by Johnny Mercer, with Tony on piano and vocals. Tony was introduced to Mercer's music during a cruise on the Royal Majesty line, which he and his mother enjoyed as guests of the cruise line company who had heard that one of Tony's wishes as a new Berklee graduate was to go on a cruise ship. Royal Majesty invited him to take a weeklong cruise and to play as many gigs as he wanted while on the trip. During that cruise, a passenger named Frank Newton, who was very taken with Tony's talent, asked to be seated at the DeBloises' dinner table each night. Newton was an avid Mercer fan and regaled Tony with stories of his genius night after night. After the trip, he mailed Tony a stack of Mercer CDs, and Tony fell in love with the songs.

The idea of a Mercer CD came up when Janice and Bill Winiker were having one of their frequent late-night phone conversations. "We both stay up late," said Janice, "and I was listing some songs that Tony liked, and it just so happened that they were all Mercer songs. As we talked, I went online to look up Johnny Mercer and found out he had written more than fifteen hundred songs, and I said to Bill, 'Mercer, mercy me!' I asked Bill what he thought about putting together a group of these songs to put on a CD, and he thought it was a good idea."

Tony also sings on the third recording he made with the Winikers, a Christmas collection named *Thrice as Nice* (2004) on which he performs on piano, vocals, and saxophone.

Tony was fifteen when he met the Winikers, and through the years Bill and Bo have witnessed the dramatic strides in his speech and language. At first Tony barely spoke but communicated with them solely through the music. Bill described Tony's gradual shift toward speech as "a flower blossoming in springtime, the way he has opened up and is so social now. He can go to any group of people and talk to them, and the second thing he does after meeting someone is take out his business card. He's just so lovable and so sweet." As Bo commented at the opening of this chapter, he and his brother consider Tony a unique voice in the jazz world. "He's developed his own vocabulary," said Bill. "That's what jazz musicians do. Tony is a high-level jazz pianist; he has a definite style, a nice modern style. He's great with harmony; I don't know how he does it. We call it juicing it up; he knows how to create really fresh harmonies behind the melodies more so than some of the other pianists I've worked with. His harmonic sense is amazing."

The Winikers have also been touched by Tony's cheerfulness; he always shows up with a positive attitude and permeates the room with his own happy glow. "Some musicians come in a little dragged, a little down, but with Tony it's like the sun is shining all around when he comes to play music," said Bill. "He could have a cold, he could be sick, but when it comes to playing music, there's never any negativity."

Bo added, "If anything, sometimes we have to muzzle him; he's ready to explode right out of the gate."

Chapter Six

ALL THAT JAZZ

"In jazz, you are the composer and the performer
at the same time. So then you not only have the
responsibility of virtuosity, you then have the
added responsibility of vision. And it's a lot easier
to become a virtuoso than it is to have vision."

—*Wynton Marsalis*

REGARDLESS OF WHO PAID FOR IT, how many
legal documents were written up about it, or how it
affected special education law, Tony's entry into Berklee
for the summer program of 1989 was a landmark event
in his life. He had the incredible good fortune to arrive
at Berklee before the retirement of the most legendary
figure at the school, John LaPorta (1920–2004), one of
the most influential jazz educators in America. From
their first one-hour lesson together, LaPorta took a special interest in Tony and began what would become a

seven-year journey together at the school. It wasn't about Tony being special because he was blind or autistic; what mattered to LaPorta was the young man's incredible ear for jazz.

LaPorta got his start playing in New York in the 1940s and was the alto saxophone player in the Woody Herman band when they made their historic Carnegie Hall concert in 1946. LaPorta's brilliant playing on clarinet and sax brought him into the recording studio and onto the stage with many of the masters: Charlie Parker, Dizzy Gillespie, Miles Davis, Duke Ellington, Gunther Schuller, Herb Pomeroy, Lester Young, and Bill Evans, to name a few. He also performed classical music as a soloist with major orchestras under conductors such as Leonard Bernstein and Leopold Stokowski.

Although he could have maintained a stellar performing career, LaPorta was attracted to teaching and enrolled in the Manhattan School of Music to get a master's degree. After graduating in 1963, he joined the Berklee faculty; and over the next thirty years, he wrote fifteen books on music education and more than two hundred compositions and recorded several of his own albums plus Music Minus One records (a standard training tool for jazz). LaPorta was nearing the end of his final decade of teaching when Tony came along.

Perhaps the best example of the high regard in which LaPorta was viewed in the music world is the story he relates in his autobiography about a rehearsal with the New York Philharmonic under Leonard Bernstein. LaPorta had been hired to play the alto saxophone part in a new composition by Teo Macero that infused a jazz quintet into a symphonic piece. During one section, LaPorta's part called for him to improvise. The strings had just finished a lush section, and LaPorta decided to start out by continuing their theme and gradually working into a jazz style that would lead into the upcoming quintet section. As he played this improvisation on the stage, the thought ran through his mind "that all my previous musical experience was a preparation for this moment." After LaPorta and the quintet finished playing that section, Bernstein stopped the orchestra and looked at LaPorta. "His face," wrote LaPorta, "full of joy, gave support to the words he uttered: 'You are a genius!' "

After hearing Tony's audition before the summer session, LaPorta was moved to go to his studio and write a thirty-two-bar instrumental in B-flat entitled "Tony's Tune," with an inscription below the title that reads: "Dedicated to Tony DeBlois." A few sharply accented eighth-note figures in the melody indicate, perhaps,

Tony's erratic body movements; while the B-flat-major key is all about exuberance. With that, LaPorta captured his first impression of the young pianist with whom he would work for the next several years.

In their first lessons together, LaPorta was astounded by Tony's ability to immediately repeat even the most complex melodies and harmonies presented to him. In the traditional jazz call-and-response style, LaPorta would play a melody on the clarinet, and Tony would repeat it on the piano; then Tony played it again with a harmonization in the left hand as LaPorta played along. LaPorta had worked with many extremely talented young students throughout his career, but Tony's speed in picking up melodies and the harmonies to support them was very unusual. "LaPorta was ecstatic about Tony," said Gregory Badolato, a Berklee faculty member. "He came to us and said, 'Wow, he's a *great* music student, I can show him *all* this stuff. . . .' "

Taken under LaPorta's wing, Tony's future at Berklee was guaranteed to be a breakthrough period in his musical life. But as everyone would soon discover, LaPorta's influence played an important role in Tony's language development, too. At Berklee, Tony came out of his shell like never before and gradually shifted from a nonreactive, disjointed speaker into a conversational young man. Tony's connection to LaPorta made an impact on his communication skills that became evident as early as that first summer session. For the first two weeks, Tony, then fifteen years old, did not use speech to react to what was going on around him, either in lessons or in the classroom. He was also nervous about being among so many students both in the classrooms and on the sidewalks of downtown Boston as he was led to the various buildings of the campus every day. The jostling clamor of students around him was almost unbearable, but he accepted that this was part of the deal, and he got used to it.

Suddenly immersed in the student population, Tony seemed to find a new voice that he had not been motivated to use before. One memorable day, he walked into LaPorta's studio and said, "John, John!" It was the first time he had shown any kind of recognition to an individual in this new environment, and LaPorta and others were moved by the fact that Tony was more aware of things outside of music than they had thought.

LaPorta's influence on Tony was one part of the impact that Berklee's unique atmosphere would have on his education, as Badolato explained.

You have to realize something about John; he was one of the oldest teachers at that time at the college. This is an old jazz man, an old jazz guy from way back who played with all the greats, all the major jazz forces.

He came to Berklee and began a lot of the improv work here. Tony had a very close relationship with John, and he was a great teacher. He approached Tony just like he approached any student: This is how you learn jazz; this is it. He treated Tony with the same love and respect as any teacher in this school. We all see a kid as a musician; that's the identity. We're all musicians here, we're no different from these kids; we have no distance except in age. In music there's no generation gap, just an age gap. John just thought Tony was a great music student.

Tony's summer session involved daily lessons with LaPorta; ear-training classes with Badolato; piano lessons, jazz piano labs, and theory with Suzanna Sifter; and ensembles. His personal aide, a young man named Adam Wannie, guided him to each class and tape-recorded each session so that Tony could work on the material at home every evening.

Sifter was surprised that she had been selected as Tony's piano teacher. At twenty-three, she had just been hired by Berklee and was finishing her last year of graduate school at the New England Conservatory. When Sifter first learned that a blind, autistic student was coming into the program, she assumed that he would be assigned to a teacher with more experience. But looking back, she realized that they probably had other factors in mind. "I think they wanted somebody who didn't have any preconceived notions about what somebody with disabilities can and can't do," she said. "As a matter of fact, through all the time I knew Tony, I never read any books about autism; I just wanted to deal with him as a person and take him from where he was and take him through our curriculum."

In Tony's first day of piano lab, Sifter noticed his unusual posture, sitting at the keyboard with one hand at his face, his thumb and forefinger pressed into his eyes. He didn't say a word, and she had no idea what to expect; but when she approached him with a musical task, he had a surprise in store. She suddenly realized that he understood the concepts and had an extraordinary facility with melody and harmony.

When I leaned over and played to him, he would play it back at three times the level of anyone else in class. He immediately soaked it up and was immediately able to use the idea that I was talking about in class. For instance, the pentatonic scale, everybody else would be writing it down and taking notes, and then all of a sudden he was able to play that and make a melody out of it and solo with it without me telling him how to solo; he just could do that because he could listen so much.

One of the big challenges people have when they come to this school is that they haven't done enough jazz listening, so they don't have a vocabulary of jazz rhythm, of melody, of structure, of how to solo, how to accompany. Since he had done that tremendous amount of listening, all I had to do was show him the scale, and he knew what to do with it, where the kid next to him might know the name of the scale, but he couldn't make music with it. Tony could do that immediately.

Tony's perfect repetition of what he heard could complicate things in his lessons. John LaPorta realized early on that if he played a wrong note, Tony would play it, too, which meant that they had to go back and learn the melody again. This occurred in Sifter's jazz lab from time to time, and although it could be disruptive, Sifter realized that it defined Tony's primary means of communication—and also revealed his sense of humor. One day, for example, she played a melody and hit a wrong note. Tony played it back just as she had played it and smiled and laughed as if it were a big joke. To Tony, she realized, music was an absolute; it was his whole world. A wrong note in a melody was inconceivable; it must be a trick. "He would continue to make the mistake as a joke," she said, "and that was one of the first ways of his relating to the whole world in the classroom. He kept doing that over and over. And I'd say, 'Tony, I hear that you're playing the B instead of the C-sharp, but remember, I made a mistake, and it's supposed to be C-sharp.' And he thought that was really funny. The other kids understood that he got that, and they were starting to relate to each other through those notes."

In a private lesson during that first summer session, Tony revealed an uncanny aspect of his talent to Sifter.

I taught him a classical piece, a Clementi sonatina, back when we were at the summer session. When I was playing it, he would echo it a second and a half later, throughout the entire piece. The two of us would play it along together. As he was playing it, he was listening to the next phrase and picking it up exactly. That's the level of playing musicians can do after a lot of playing, but he could do it immediately. That was a really poignant moment; I thought, "Wow, there's really something going on here."

At the end of the five-week program, fifteen-year-old Tony joined in the final concert as the pianist in an ensemble. While waiting his turn, he sat in the audience, snuggling up with his mom. When it came time for Tony to join the band, Sifter went to him and led him up to the stage. The students who had been in contact with Tony knew that he was very quiet, and everyone wondered what to expect as they watched him walk toward the piano with his light, childlike step. Could he really play? "When he got up there, he lit the piano on fire," said Sifter. "The audience really responded to him." To witness Tony's totally different persona, to see the incongruity of his disabilities and his talent firsthand, is a profound experience. As Sifter watched, she imagined that Tony was making a new connection about his gift: "What I'm assuming is he may have been thinking, 'Wow, there's a whole world out there, the people like me, I can do this, and I can relate to people through this.' "

✵ One year later, Tony attended the next five-week summer session at Berklee; and when he performed with his Rivers jazz ensemble at Berklee's 1991 High School Jazz Festival, the ensemble took second place in the overall competition. This earned the school a one-thousand-dollar scholarship that they could award to any student they chose, and Rivers awarded the scholarship to Tony. As a result, Janice met with Rob Rose, director of Berklee's special programs, to discuss the possibility of Tony enrolling in Berklee's regular college program.

Berklee was going through an adjustment period after a suit that had been made against them in 1989, in which a blind applicant who had been denied admission sued on the grounds of discrimination. Berklee had denied her application because their entrance requirements demanded that the student could sight-read. Sight-reading was a basic skill for professional musicians, they argued, because they would be called upon to do so in a variety of situations, including studio recording. The blind student filed the suit through the Office of Civil Rights of the US Department of Education, and in 1989, the two parties came to a settlement. Thereafter, Berklee revised its admissions requirements and began working on new curriculum that would allow students to compensate for sight-reading credits through other coursework. The settlement opened the door for more blind students to enroll, and although Berklee was prepared to meet these new challenges, it was still new turf.

Janice's Journal

When we talked about enrolling in the college, their question to me was, "Why do you want Tony to go to Berklee?" I told them that every vocation has its own language, and for Tony to be accepted as a musician, he had to know the language of musicians. By playing in ensembles, he would get that language.

Because Tony was talking about I-IV-V chords, some terms they use—I didn't understand, but the teachers seemed to know exactly what he was talking about—I knew that this was a language he could understand. I told them that a diploma from Berklee would open doors, that if he could walk up to a band and say he went to Berklee, that would be enough to allow him to play in a band. I felt that because Tony knew so much about music and the fact that at any given time there are people speaking, like, fifty different languages at Berklee, that people would be willing to go through all the communication barriers, including Tony's noncommunication. To me, it was clear that the one thing that was the same for everybody was music.

Ultimately, Berklee was willing to work through the communication. They had already seen how the summer program students benefited from him— pianists would just gather around to watch how he did it.

Like the new scholarship, the 1989 ruling from the hearing officer that made the Berklee summer program a valid part of Tony's IEP also opened doors. When Janice proposed to the Waltham school district that they cover Tony's tuition as a college student at Berklee, she had the 1989 arguments about the validity of Berklee training on her side. In an effort to make college courses at Berklee part of Tony's IEP, Janice first completed an application for Berklee that would enable him to enroll as a freshman in June 1992. Berklee had already awarded him a one-thousand-dollar scholarship for that twelve-week semester, which would help defray the costs for the school district. In her correspondence with the Waltham Public Schools' director of special education, Janice explained that Berklee was the most appropriate choice for Tony's vocational education because his vocational goal was to be a professional musician. "I must insist that Tony's vocational education program be in a setting with teachers who are professional musicians and with students who are pursuing careers as professional musicians," she wrote.

With the assistance of Boston's Disability Law Center, Janice successfully integrated a full-time Berklee College diploma program into Tony's IEP. The school district found a way to make his college courses a legitimate part of his public school program by having the Perkins School for the Blind subcontract Berklee College for the courses. Waltham Public Schools was already subcontracting Perkins as part of Tony's IEP, and they made it possible for Perkins to subcontract Berklee. "There are ways to go around the system to make things happen," said Janice. "If you want to obtain the best opportunities for your child, you must be creative with your problem solving."

In June 1992, Tony officially enrolled as a college student at the Berklee College of Music. As Janice thought about her seventeen-year-old walking along Boylston Street with his aide on the first day of class, she thought, "Yes! Tony is in college!" He hadn't graduated from eighth grade, he hadn't graduated from high school, but he was now in a real, regular college. For most of Tony's life, she had accepted the fact that he probably wouldn't get a high school diploma, wouldn't get a regular job, and certainly wouldn't go to college. But there he was, backpack and all, on his way to bigger things.

In college, Tony continued to work with LaPorta, Sifter, and Badolato, and he also took up voice lessons with Sharon Brown. He was still a student at Perkins, too, where he began taking violin lessons with Arnie Harris. Badolato, who chaired the ear-training department at Berklee, taught Tony himself throughout the four required semesters of the subject, and he was surprised at the ease with which Tony learned solfege.

Ear training is taught with solfege here [labeling pitches with a syllable rather than with the letter-name of the pitch: do re mi fa sol la ti do]. So in any key, do is the key. That's what Tony had to learn. He wasn't able to read because he didn't have Braille, so we made it harder on the dictation and the identification side.

He would sit in class, and he had his aide with him, and I would sing the examples, and he would learn them, memorize them, and sing them. He then did exercises where I would attach the syllables to the notes. If I gave him an interval, do-fa [singing], he would learn how to identify a perfect fourth with those syllable names. Tony would also have to sing a melody back to me and identify it in solfege syllables. That would tell me that he knew what it was, just as other music students would do.

I don't know the scientific explanation of cognitive understanding, but I know that he was able to do this. I'd play something on the piano, and he'd sing it back: do-fa-mi-re-do-la-sol-fa-mi-re-do, and to me that's a linkage of sound and identification. That's what we ask all music students to do.

Rob Rose added, "That's actually grasping a very serious concept to be able to do that. It's not like playing it back on the keyboard; to put pitches together with the syllables, that's serious. He's putting two things together."

In an NBC *Today Show* segment on Tony that aired in 1991, Tony was introduced as one of seven musical savants alive in the world today, and footage showed him playing in a jazz ensemble classroom at Berklee. One student interviewed for the segment described Tony as a musician "who's not really hung up on the technical part. It comes from inside of him, and it just comes right out on the keys; you can tell; you can feel it." A guitar player added, "He's one cool cat, that's all I've got to say," and a third student said, "When he starts it jammin' here, it always works because he just starts it with so much energy, it's contagious."

The *Today Show* segment included an interview with Tony conducted by Dr. Treffert, who explained that "Many savants speak just like they play, which means they're very literal; it's rote, and it's played back exactly as it's heard. *He* improvises."

Tony's ability to improvise rather than simply echo music he hears is one of two startling points about his playing. The second issue involves the *way* he plays: As an autistic, one would expect his playing to be mechanical, stiff, and devoid of emotion. Three minutes into his CD *Beyond Words*, however, the listener hears the subtlety, sophistication, and refined musicality of a true artist. It is amazing enough that Tony has the technical capacity to play Beethoven sonatas and complex jazz harmonies; it is even more spectacular that he plays with the depth and nuance of a seasoned professional. This is the type of playing that moved John LaPorta to believe that Tony had all the resources to become an important voice in American jazz. As all of Tony's Berklee teachers observed, Tony was such a sponge of sound that he even adjusted his playing to the group he was with. This phenomenon was another mysterious dimension of his savant skills, revealed in the fact that at Berklee he played at an extraordinarily high level with a highly skilled group but could also turn around and play like any college kid in a mediocre ensemble. "It was very evident that if he was with real good players, he was playing really good," said Rose. "If he was playing with lower-level people, he wouldn't play as well. He was like two different people."

Professional jazz musicians may vary their playing according to the logistics of the performance space and other factors, and Tony did this, as well. "You have to edit yourself and play according to the level of the sound, how much energy you can put out, how complicated the ideas can be," said Badolato. "When you hear Tony onstage, he's playing to the gig. He plays to the level of performers around him, but it's the gig, too."

✻ Even before Tony began to have national recognition on TV shows such as the *Today Show, Strange Science,* and *Entertainment Tonight,* his charms caught him a girlfriend who today is one of his best friends. Cydnie Breazeale-Davis was a fellow student at Perkins, a pianist, and was hearing impaired as well as blind. Tony invited Cydnie to the junior prom, but she already had a date. Tony took someone else to the dance, but he hung around with Cydnie most of the night. In a photo of that event, Tony is standing next to his date but holding hands with Cydnie. That night, Cydnie asked Tony to take her to the prom the following year, and he did. Cydnie would be completely deaf without her cochlear implant, but she hears well enough with this device to go to school, talk on the telephone, and play jazz piano in an ensemble. Now and then, she and her mother go to Skipjack's on a Sunday so that Cydnie can take Tony's seat at the piano and give him a chance to play the saxophone and trumpet with the Winiker Quartet. Tony studies trumpet with Bo Winiker and is extremely proud to be able to perform as an instrumentalist as well as a pianist in the group.

Since Tony and Cydnie first met, they've spent most Tuesday evenings at Tony's house jamming together and talking about school and music. Tony takes Cydnie out for dinner at their favorite seafood restaurant and also calls her to meet up for coffee and doughnuts. "Tony is a good dancer," Cydnie said in a phone interview. "He can take me out. We like to go for seafood, and we like to go to Dunkin' Donuts the best."

Once Tony was in college, Janice's schedule was packed with driving him to wherever he needed to go, from his visits with Cydnie to his private lessons and weekend gigs all over New England. Janice talked about the scheduling demands of raising Tony when she met Henry David Feldman, a professor at Tufts University who has written several books about gifted children. As they discussed some of the points he had made over the years about the extra work parents assumed in raising a gifted child, Janice asked, "Yes, but what about when your child is gifted *and* special needs?" Janice explained that she was constantly driving Tony to various special needs programs, taking him to concerts so he could hear other people playing music, and trying to do other things with his life such as swimming and museum visits so that he would be a well-rounded child.

On the weekends when Tony didn't have a performance, Janice often took him and Ray to activities organized by the Alternative Leisure Company, which offered outings for children and adults with special needs. Through this organization, the boys went swimming, ice skating, horseback riding, and roller skating and attended puppet shows. The family's schedule became more hectic when Tony began to schedule more national performances. One weekend, for example, Janice flew out of town on Friday afternoon to take Tony to his performance at the Variety Club of Southern California's telethon. They flew back on Sunday and only got a few hours' sleep, as Janice had to be at work and Tony had to be at class at eight o'clock Monday morning.

From 1988 to 1995, Janice managed this schedule while working full-time as a business administrator at the Spire Corporation in Bedford, Massachusetts. Spire manufactured solar panels, flat-screen televisions, and other products; and Janice ran into problems at each of her annual reviews when her boss complained about the time she had to take off to take Tony or Ray somewhere, attend an IEP meeting, or deal with some other matter related to their care. Janice had made it very clear before accepting the job that she would be gone from time to time due to these commitments, and management had agreed to hire her and promised, as she requested, not to factor those absences into her annual performance reviews. Nevertheless, the topic always came up during those reviews. After Tony got into Berklee College for the diploma program, Janice informed the company that she would leave in a few years, after he graduated. In December 1995, six months before Tony's graduation, Janice's boss once again discussed her absences at her review. She had had enough and gave her notice that day.

Two days after Tony appeared on the *Today Show*, Janice got a call from a movie producer named Tyler Tyhurst who had seen the show. "Tyler called me up and said, 'I rarely watch TV, and I was getting dressed this morning and saw this story, and I want to make it into a movie,' " Janice said. "It was quite a shock." Tyhurst and his partner, Jim Knoll, owned Tyhurst Productions, and the project went through years of development before finally being picked up by CBS for production as a Movie of the Week. When CBS finally made the deal, they hired Dalene Young, a twenty-year veteran of Hollywood television screenwriting, to adapt Tony's story for TV. Her material came directly from Tyhurst, who had gathered the facts through long conversations with Janice over the years. Filming began in April 1996, with Cybill Shepherd playing the role of Janice and Chris Demetral as Tony. Director Karen Arthur, another Hollywood veteran who had directed scores of TV movies as well as TV series including *Cagney & Lacy*, *Hart to Hart*, and *Remington Steele*, finished filming in three months.

Janice, Tom, Ray, and Tony visited the set for five

days, and Tony was fascinated by the actors' rehearsals he overheard in the hallway. When an assistant director read the lines, Tony instantly memorized them. Later, wearing headphones that allowed him to hear the filming on the set, Tony was confounded that the actors couldn't remember some of their lines. Janice had to laugh when he slipped off his headphones one morning and asked, "Can't they get it right?"

Tony appeared briefly in the last scene of the movie, and he also played five songs on the soundtrack. *Journey of the Heart* debuted on CBS on March 2, 1997. When Janice saw the final version, she was overcome with pride to have Tony brought to a national audience. At the same time, she was more than startled by the liberties that the screenwriter had taken with the facts. Tony's girlfriend, for example, was portrayed as a perfectly normal, pretty blonde. Janice hoped that someday she would have the opportunity to tell the whole, real story to a large audience. Sadly, Janice's friend and producer Tyler Tyhurst died shortly before the film was completed. "He got a cold and passed away from AIDS," said Janice. "If you watch the movie, you'll see it was dedicated to him." The movie continues to air on the Lifetime television network in 2005.

❧ In the spring of 1996, Tony was twenty-two years old and excited about his impending graduation from Berklee. The family was busy planning the graduation party, Tony had new music to practice for a special graduation concert, and Ray was being evaluated for a new residential special education facility called the Eagleton School. There were many bright things to look forward to, but two unhappy events were about to unfold.

Janice and Tom's nine-year marriage had been challenged by many things, including Ray's disabilities, which brought on a seemingly endless series of behavioral problems and scrapes with the law. They had seen a marriage counselor and worked hard on the relationship; but in July, two months after Tony's graduation, Janice received a "Dear Jan" letter that heralded the end of the marriage. For five pages, Tom declared his devotion to the boys but admitted that he felt that he and Janice had moved too fast. Janice knew more than anyone that parenting two disabled children took enormous strength, patience, and self-sacrifice; and she realized it wasn't a job for just anyone. But with both Owen and Tom, she had believed, for a while, that they were up to the task.

Tom moved out on June 14, two days before Father's Day and four days before their ninth wedding anniversary. Their divorce was finalized on their anniversary the following year.

Ray had grown very attached to Tom and thought about him much more than Janice knew. This became clear after another dramatic episode with Ray, this time of tragic proportions.

On a crisp autumn day in September 1997, seventeen-year-old Ray went on a supervised hiking trip with a small group of students from the Eagleton School. As they walked through the glorious colors of the Berkshires near the Appalachian Trail, they came to a steep ridge, and Ray lost his footing. He fell forty-two feet, breaking several bones, including three vertebrae in his back. A military helicopter airlifted Ray to Albany Medical Center in nearby Albany, New York. By the time Janice arrived, the emergency doctors had sedated him into unconsciousness to spare him the pain.

When Janice got to the emergency room, one doctor was sewing Ray's scalp back to his head and another doctor was arranging x-rays on a screen to show Ray's fractures to Janice. His right shoulder and collarbone were broken to the extent that he needed an iron rod to connect his arm to his shoulder. His T2 and T4 (thoracic) vertebrae were fractured, and the T3 was completely shattered. In the next four weeks, Ray would undergo five surgeries to set the pin in his arm and rebuild his spine with another steel rod to extend from vertebrae T1 to T5.

The doctors were reluctant to break the news to Janice that Ray was paralyzed and would never walk again. She insisted on hearing the truth and reacted just as she had when she learned that Tony was permanently blind. Rather than grieve over this tragic news, she got practical. "I kept pushing the doctors," said Janice. "I told them that I needed to know whether he was going to be paralyzed and how long he would require physical rehabilitation because his school situation had to be addressed. I had to find a school that was accessible and also find tutors for him in the meantime. It would change his whole education plan." Janice also had no time for the visitors who took her hand and expressed their pity for her situation. "It struck me as odd that people would come up to me and say, 'You poor thing, what else can happen to you?' I'd have to remind them that this didn't happen to me, it happened to Ray."

After recovering from all of his surgeries, Ray was transferred to the HealthSouth New England Rehabilitation Hospital in Boston for two months. He then returned to Eagleton School, which had become completely accessible since his accident with ramps and other renovations. Janice wanted Ray to return to the school so that he could see his friends and come to some closure with the place. The car trip from Boston to Eagleton started out smoothly enough, but within a short time it evolved into an all-day ordeal that provided one more example of the challenges that continually popped up in spite of Janice's best-laid plans.

Janice's Journal

Ray returned to Eagleton the year after his accident, and on the drive from the hospital to the school along Interstate 90, I had made arrangements to pick up his wheelchair from the people who sold it to us. We were supposed to meet these people by a tollbooth, and they were going to show me how to operate it. We met up just fine and got the wheelchair and the transfer board on which Ray would slide in and out of the chair. This transfer board looked like a white plastic cutting board; it was only about fourteen inches wide. It wasn't nearly long enough for him to reach from the car seat to the wheelchair.

We had planned to stop at a restaurant to celebrate Tony's birthday on the way, but we had to find a bigger board first. First, we asked at the tollbooth whether they knew of a medical supply place; but this was western Massachusetts, and they said there was nothing out there. Then, when we got back on the interstate, we saw a state trooper pulling someone over, so we stopped and asked him if he had a transfer board. He didn't, but he suggested we call the fire department. They couldn't help either, so I contacted a staff person from Eagleton who was a volunteer EMT. That night, some guys in the shop at the school made Ray a perfectly sized transfer board.

God rides on our shoulder; every time we've ever needed anything, He's been right there.

It was difficult for Ray to get continuity at Eagleton because he spent a lot of time being transported to his physical therapy and doctors' visits. Eagleton was located far from these services, and the trips cut into Ray's class time. This problem led to Ray's evaluation for placement at the Crotched Mountain School and Rehabilitation Center in Greenfield, New Hampshire. After a few months at Crotched Mountain, Ray went through another lengthy evaluation to be placed at the Lakeview Neuro-Rehabilitation Center in Effingham Falls, New Hampshire.

Ray loved animals; and Lakeview gave him the opportunity to work with the sheep, goats, and horse that pastured around the facility and lived in the barn. "My job was to feed them and to clean out their stalls," Ray said. He couldn't brush the horse because the animal was "a little skittish of my wheelchair—at that time I only had a manual." Ray also loved working in the greenhouse and some of the other activities at Lakeview. "In the greenhouse I watered the plants, made new plants doing the seeds, changed a plant from a small pot to a bigger pot," he said. "I also worked in the wood shop, fixed any of the tables or chairs that were broken."

Ray inherited his mother and grandfather's talent for electronics; and since moving home at age twenty-two, he has taken up fix-it jobs around the house. "Anything that breaks over here now that's electrical, I'm fixing it," he said. "I rewired a lamp that Mom had gotten, I teach Mom how to use the cell phone, teach her how to use the digital camera. With Tony's TV/VCR combo, I was the one that was doing the taping if we were making a copy because I knew how to run it. If you come to me with a problem, something electrical, I'm able to figure out how to make it work. I'm also the one who knows all the routes to the bus and the subway and the commuter rail."

Janice's house in Waltham was too small to be made accessible, so in August 2000, she and Ray bought a one-story ranch in Randolph, a southern suburb of Boston near Braintree. When she began creating a chronological scrapbook of Tony's performances and awards a couple of years later, she looked into her family history and learned about Benjamin Allbee and his beginnings in Braintree. It was an astonishing twist of fate to be so near her earliest American roots, and she enjoyed telling Tony and Ray stories about Allbee's contributions to the area and about his adventurous final years.

❦ A year after his accident, Ray had become accustomed to getting around in his large motorized wheelchair and to using the Randolph bus system to go to the barber shop and to Dunkin' Donuts with Tony. Living in his own apartment on one side of the house, Ray could call a handicapped transportation service to schedule a ride. In the summertime, he and Tony got around town very well. Tony walked behind the wheelchair, with Ray as his guide.

Ray continued to have behavioral problems due to Asperger's and Klinefelter's syndromes, however, and he still managed to run away from home in spite of his new handicap. In 2002, he went missing for two days, and Janice made frantic phone calls trying to find him. She finally tracked him down at a hospital, where he had checked himself in for a urinary tract infection. The nurse told her that he had checked out and requested a wheelchair-capable van, or "chair car" service, to take him to his father's house in Woburn. Just after Janice hung up the phone, Ray showed up in the chair car and came into the house. He told Janice that he had gone to Tom's house, but he was obviously crushed by the cool reception. Janice realized for the first time how much he had been missing his stepfather.

Janice's Journal

Church has been an important part of our lives for a long time. It's really strange because it's almost like Tony absorbed God. Prayer isn't something that he does at certain times of the day. If a friend tells Tony that he's sick, he stops what he's doing right then and says three Hail Marys for him. When I was sick and missed church choir practice one night, some choir friends told me later that Tony and Ray had both asked everybody to say prayers for me.

Shortly after we moved to Stoneham, we began going to Sunday evening Faith and Light services. This is a program run by some of the Catholic churches for people with disabilities. It was attended by parents and their special-needs kids; and everyone would bring something to eat, and we'd have music and skits and other things.

After I married Tom, I converted to Catholicism; and to prepare for that, I attended Adult Initiation classes at St. Patrick's Church in Stoneham. A member of St. Charles Catholic Church of Waltham came to the house to instruct Tony, and Tom gave Ray classes at Our Lady Comforter of the Afflicted Church in Waltham. Tony was really interested in what was going on. We also went to weekly Bible study, and Tony's favorite Bible passage became, "When the blind lead the blind, they fall into the ditch." He thinks that's really funny. We read the New Way version of the Bible; and when we were at Bible study one night, Ray was asked to read part of the Book of Revelation that talks about the end of the world coming. While he was reading, he said, "And there were no pianos and no saxophones," and he looked over at Tony. Father Mike said to Ray, "Does it really say that?" Holding the Bible out, Ray said, "Honest, Father Mike!" We all thought about it for a second, then everyone burst out laughing.

Because of Tony's ability to memorize, he got the Mass down great; he knows all the prayers. Ray was an altar server for a while, and I was a Eucharistic minister, giving out the consecrated host during communion. Now we sing in the choir at St. Mary's in Randolph.

The first year that Tony played at the Fatima

Shrine in Alexandria, South Dakota, when he was twenty-four years old, we got the keyboard all set up to play the prelude before the Mass. Three thousand people were there. It started to rain, which was going to wreak havoc with our equipment. In front of all those people, Tony said into the microphone, "God, please make it stop raining." It stopped raining, and Tony started his prelude.

Janice had made the decision to put religious faith at the heart of her family when Tony was just a baby in Texas. Tony's strong bond with his mother has led him to embrace this aspect of their lives with the innocent, open-hearted enthusiasm that he brings to music and to the friendships he has made with the people who are close to the family. In the process, Tony has found his own faith, which Janice sees him draw upon as he prays for people who need help.

Through the years that Tony worked closely with his fellow musicians at the music school at Rivers and at Berklee, he revealed more of his personality and showed a strength of character that had been unimaginable when he was a child. In his preteen years in Texas and South Dakota, Tony appeared to be enclosed in a shell that could not be broken other than through the piano playing that others could enjoy. But the interaction with young musicians that began in Massachusetts broke down language and communication barriers to gradually reveal the person beneath the autistic disability. By the time Tony graduated from Berklee, he was respected and admired by classmates and teachers as an exceptional musician.

LEGACY *of* LOVE

"Each man has his own music
bubbling up inside him."

—*Louis Armstrong*

THE HYNES CONVENTION CENTER in Boston
was packed on May 12, 1996, for Berklee College's Sunday afternoon graduation ceremony. Five hundred graduates filled the center seats, surrounded by a crowd of three thousand friends and family. When Berklee president Lee Berk called out the name "Tony DeBlois," the crowd jumped to its feet and burst into shouts of applause. Gown flowing, a shining medallion hanging from his neck, Tony walked across the stage to shake hands with Berk and receive his diploma. Tony was awarded Berklee's Fifty-Year Anniversary Medallion in recognition of him as "most improved student." Diploma in hand, Tony stepped over to shake hands with

jazz guitarist Pat Metheny and singer Patti LaBelle, both of whom received honorary degrees that day. With a grade-point average above 3.5, Tony graduated *magna cum laude* at age twenty-two and made the history books as the first blind, autistic savant to graduate from the Berklee College of Music.

After the ceremony, one of the local TV reporters covering the event asked Tony, "Are you proud of yourself today?" Tony answered, "I am proud; I am definitely proud."

The night before, Tony was among the graduates performing at the special concert held in honor of Metheny and LaBelle. Tony played a piano solo for the crowd at the twelve-hundred-seat Berklee Performance Center; and after the concert, he got a personal visit from his newest fan. All the student performers waited in the greenroom to meet the two honorees. When LaBelle swept through the door, she asked, "Where is Tony DeBlois? I have to give that Tony DeBlois a great big kiss!" Much to Tony's delight, she took his face in her hands and planted a big kiss on his cheek.

Tony's graduation party at home on Washington Avenue in Waltham that night was a rock 'n' roll blowout. The previous year, Tony had joined a rock band named Wooden Nickels, and Janice invited the band to set up in the backyard and play for the party.

Tony joined the band after his brother told Janice one day about an ad he found in the *New England Performer.* Ray looked up from the paper and called out to his mom, "Here's something I bet you won't let Tony do!" Janice read the ad herself and called the band, then they drove out to hear Tony and called back a day later to offer him the job. They entertained the whole neighborhood during Tony's party—and then some. People who heard the band while driving down busy Moody Street parked their cars and walked toward the music. This created a traffic jam and forced the police to drive out to the house and shut down the band. When they arrived, some of Janice's friends tried to convince them to let the music go on, explaining Tony's story, his notoriety as a savant, and his incredible feat in graduating. The police were happy for him, but they had to do their job. Tony got a chance to visit with more of the guests after the band quit, and in spite of the shutdown order from the police, it was a great night.

Tony's life took a new direction after graduation, with many more performances out of town, out of state, and out of the country. At home, Tony lived as independently as possible in his own apartment located in the rear section of the house, and he settled into a new weekly routine that he holds to this day. The apartment includes a kitchen, a music practice area, and a bedroom with a TV close to the bed. Ray's apartment, which is somewhat larger, is on the other side of the house.

Each day begins with Tony waking up before anyone else and making a cup of coffee for his mom. He puts a single coffee packet into a cup of water, heats it up in the microwave, and brings it to her in bed. They snuggle and talk for a few minutes, then Tony's personal attendant arrives to help him with his shower and shaving. On Tuesday mornings Tony has a trumpet lesson with Bo Winiker, and on Tuesday evenings he visits with his girl-friend, Cydnie, at her house or his. On Wednesday nights Tony goes to choir practice at St. Mary's with his mom and Ray, who also sing in the choir. Every Thursday afternoon, Tony has coffee with his friend Bill Conroy from church, a retired postal worker who loves to sing through hymns and show tunes while Tony accompanies on the piano. Some weeks, they leave the music behind and just take a walk in the woods and talk. On many weeknights, Tony is also scheduled to perform at an event, and weekends are often taken up with perfor-mances at conventions and other large-scale venues out of town. When Tony is at home, Sunday mornings are spent singing in choir at church, and once a month he plays with the Winiker Jazz Quartet on Sunday after-noons at Skipjack's.

Although Tony can chat with fans and sign autographs after a gig, take the bus around town with his
brother, hold interviews with the media, focus intently
on recordings of music he needs to learn, and perform
like a pro on stage, there are many things he cannot do,
and it is impossible for him to live on his own. Janice has
described him as "a man-child" with adult abilities in
some areas and very childlike or no ability at all in others. Tony learned how to button the large buttons on his
pajamas at age twenty-six, how to button his tuxedo shirt
buttons at age twenty-seven, and how to buckle his belt
at twenty-eight. Although Tony's fingers are precise and
nimble at the keyboard, he cannot tie his shoes, and his
attention span is not long enough to enable him to walk
across the street by himself. When Janice brings Tony to
schools to play for students of all ages, she tells them
about the years of struggle Tony went through to learn
how to button his shirt and make her a cup of coffee.
"We tell the kids that you're never too old to learn, and
practice, practice, practice," Janice said.

As word about Tony has spread throughout the
Boston area, the East Coast, and across the country, he's
been invited to play for many events and has built up a
repertoire of approximately eight thousand songs,
according to Janice's latest estimation. Tony loves to sing
at the piano and memorizes the nuances of foreign lan-

guages as quickly and easily as English. After trips to Singapore and Taiwan, for example, where Tony heard many Asian-language songs on the radio, he memorized a song in Taiwanese that he particularly enjoyed. He also sings songs in French, German, Spanish, Swahili, and Italian. When Tony visited Boston mayor Tom Menino in November 2003, he very appropriately chose to sing "Santa Lucia," a song in Italian about the patron saint of the blind. Tony also played the mayor's favorite song, "My Way," singing his own version of the lyrics: "I did it God's way."

Menino, who had invited Tony for this visit after reading about him in a *Boston Globe* article, was moved to say, "We have people who complain about the smallest little things. This kid's born one pound, keeps overcoming obstacles, and I can't say the right words to express my feelings. I've had good days and bad days, but today is one of the best days of my career." When Tony was introduced to Menino that day, he told him that he'd really like to play at the upcoming Democratic National Convention in Boston. After saying this, he quickly slipped something out of his pocket and added, "Here's my card." Menino laughed and thanked him, and he and the journalists who observed this exchange were completely won over. Menino made good on the request and arranged for Tony to perform at a private party hosted by himself and Senator Ted Kennedy at the Parkman House during the convention.

Since the early 1990s, Tony has performed throughout the United States at events for organizations such as the International Special Olympics, Variety Club International, the International Council on Autism, the National Autism Society of America, and Very Special Arts (VSA), for whom he has played a number of events including the VSA twenty-fifth anniversary concert at the John F. Kennedy Center for the Performing Arts in Washington, DC. In New England alone, Tony has made more than two hundred appearances in a wide variety of venues, from a performance at the Diocesan Celebration for Persons with Disabilities at Boston's Cathedral of the Holy Cross to the opening ceremonies of McCoy Stadium in Pawtucket, Rhode Island.

Many of Tony's invitations to perform occurred after he was awarded the Very Special Arts Itzhak Perlman Award in 1992. This award, sponsored by Panasonic, is given annually to an outstanding performing artist with a disability under the age of twenty-one. Perlman, one of the greatest violinists of our time, was struck by polio at the age of four; since then, he has walked with crutches and played the violin while sitting down. In spite of Perlman's lifelong disability, he is one of the luminaries of classical music.

Another major award that recognized Tony's accomplishments was the 1996 Reynolds Society Achievement Award, named for the cofounder of the Massachusetts Eye and Ear Infirmary. Each year, this award is presented to "individuals challenged by the loss of vision, hearing, or speech who have achieved a noteworthy level of excellence in their field, and individuals whose contributions and innovations have enabled others so challenged to lead more active and independent lives." The other two artists who received the award in 1996 were the renowned deaf percussionist Evelyn Glennie from Scotland and visually impaired American photographer George A. Covington.

In 1993, Tony was recognized by the Foundation for Exceptional Children with their "Yes, I Can" Award; and in 2000, he received the Faith and Family Foundation Outstanding Achievement Award, presented by Irish tenor Mark Forrest. Forrest and his wife are the parents of a blind and disabled son, and their award led to Tony's participation in a concert at Dublin's National Concert Hall in 2004. The previous year, Tony was named one of the Boston Celtics' "Heroes Among Us," a recognition given to those "who have made an overwhelming impact on our community, positively affecting the lives of others." The basketball team announces an awardee at each home game; and at the FleetCenter in November 2003,

Tony went to center court to receive the award and sing "The Star Spangled Banner" before a raucously adoring crowd. "Everyone was cheering, whistling, and clapping," Tony said after the game.

The press coverage of all of these awards has brought Tony international recognition, and events throughout the world in which he has performed include the Catholic Church's World Youth Day 2002, held in Toronto, Canada. Held every two years, this event was founded by Pope John Paul II to bring people ages sixteen to thirty-five together to share their faith, celebrate Mass with him, pray together, and enjoy music and film. Catholic churches throughout the world received a letter from the Pope the previous year, in which he invited youth to attend and introduced the theme for the upcoming year's celebration: "You are the salt of the earth, the light of the world." Part of that letter urged young people to aim high with their gifts, a message that tied in closely to the theme of Tony's concerts for schoolchildren.

It is the nature of human beings, and especially youth, to seek the Absolute, the meaning and fullness of life. Dear young people, do not be content with anything less than the highest ideals! Do not let yourselves be dispirited by those who are disillusioned with life and have grown deaf to the deepest and most authentic desires of their heart. You are right to be disappointed with hollow entertainment and passing fads, and with aiming at too little in life. If you have an ardent desire for the Lord, you will steer clear of the mediocrity and conformism so widespread in our society.

These ideas matched those that Tony shared with students grades K through 12 at his school concerts, in which he sang and played songs and talked about the importance of following your dreams. "He tells the kids to have high hopes, to not give up on their dreams, and that it's okay to be different," said Janice. "He starts each program with twenty minutes of songs that retell his own story, in a way, such as "Johnny Be Good," which is about a boy who can't read or write very well but who grows up to lead a rock 'n' roll band. The students ask a lot of questions, and they go away very inspired about what they can do."

Tony performed during the weeklong event in July and had the opportunity to hear the Pope celebrate Mass.

Tony's most distant trip thus far has been to Singapore, where he played a fund-raiser for the Reach-Me Project. His performance raised $250,000 at the charity's black-tie dinner-dance at the Singapore Ritz-Carlton in October 1998. Tony returned to Singapore in January

2002 to perform at the International Festival for the Supra-Senses, which was held at Singapore's famous Chijmes Hall. In addition to the festival performances, Tony was invited to sit in every night with combos at the Somerset Jazz Club. "They love Tony in Singapore," Janice said.

The VSA award brought Tony to the attention of the Millennium Stage, a concert series that provides free daily performances in the Millennium Stage Grand Foyer of the Kennedy Center for the Performing Arts. A video clip of Tony's thundering performance of Gershwin's "Rhapsody in Blue" in July 2000 for this series can be found at the Web site listed on page 237.

≪ Tony loves performing everywhere and anywhere, and his focus on music above and beyond every other activity in his life represents the element of savant syndrome that Dr. Treffert describes as an obsessive relationship with the skill. In Tony's case, this focus has brought great rewards in several aspects of his life, including his ability not only to relate to the world but to contribute to it, as well. To Janice, Tony's vocation as a professional musician has taken him out of the traditional realm of people with severe disabilities and made him "a tax-paying rather than a tax-taking citizen."

As a hard-working, tax-paying musician, Tony is never

at a loss for work. Rather than seek out performing opportunities, Janice constantly receives calls from people who want to engage Tony because they heard about him through his performances, the Web site, the TV movie, or other media. The requests come almost daily from individuals and organizations, and Tony normally has a full schedule four or five months in advance. "There isn't a whole lot of room to plan far in advance," said Janice. "There's so much that just comes at us, and we go wherever that takes us." In addition to Tony's many performances, his goal is to continue to record a new CD every year; and he would also like to be interviewed on TV by Ellen DeGeneres and Katie Couric, play for the president of the United States, and perform on Broadway, at Carnegie Hall, and with the Boston Pops.

❧ In terms of Tony's greatest happiness, all of the awards, television programs, media recognition, and even performances are secondary to the real love of his life. Tony and his mother have a deep bond that is obvious at first glance, a bond that does not reflect any of the unemotional, unaffectionate traits that are normally attributed to autism. Janice strives to give Tony as much independence as possible, from running around town with his brother and having his own checking account to choosing a restaurant for dinner and drawing out his own spending money from the local bank's talking ATM. These activities may seem mundane, but for a young man who spent his entire childhood locked in an inner world with no ability to grasp the simple pleasures of life, these are the things that make every day fresh and magical.

Janice knows that Tony still depends on her for many aspects of his day-to-day life, but she also knows that he, like all children, is here on his own journey. It is a mysterious journey that neither Janice nor music educators nor psychiatrists will ever understand, as it is part of the mystery of humankind. As Kahlil Gibran wrote, "Your children are not your children. / They are the sons and daughters of Life's longing for itself."

Janice's Journal

What better legacy of love can we give our children than a life that can be led as independently and meaningfully as possible? Being of pioneer spirit, I believe I have looked to the future with a purposeful vision, put one foot in front of the other, and learned with each step that I have taken. I had the hangup of having been born in 1946, when the United States had just emerged from World War II, and it was thought to be unpatriotic if you ever thought the government could be wrong. I am a Vietnam-era veteran and served two and a half years during that war; I am one of those who started to question the interpretation of the law and especially school officials who were doing the interpreting for me. It was then that I decided to see whether their or my interpretation would stand up in a court of law. Today, I ask parents to look to the future not only for their sake but also and especially for the sake of their children.

As John F. Kennedy said, "Children are our greatest natural resource." We must remember to keep our options open, to learn from our mistakes, and to build the best possible foundation for our children in our homes, our schools, and our hearts.

NOTES

For further information on the book titles, please see the Suggested Reading section on page 237.

Prelude

xiii *Within that group* Darold A. Treffert, MD, *Extraordinary People: Understanding Savant Syndrome* Lincoln, NE: iUniverse.com, 2000), 16.

Chapter Two

57 *Development chart* Middle-column portions extracted from National Center on Birth Defects and Developmental Disabilities Web site (www.cdc.gov/ncbddd/autism/actearly).

Chapter Three

82 *"We cannot simply . . ."* Darold A. Treffert, MD, *Extraordinary People: Understanding Savant Syndrome,* 14.

83 *Approximately 10 percent* "Savant Syndrome: 'Special Faculties' Extraordinaire," *Psychiatric Times* (October 2001), 20.

84 *Dr. Down's brief initial description* Darold A. Treffert, MD, *Extraordinary People: Understanding Savant Syndrome,* 23.

85 *Some savants could tell* Ibid., 25.

87 *He introduced himself* Ibid., 40.

88 *After that, he forced* Ibid., 38–39.

88 *"Whether in his improvisations . . ."* Savant syndrome Web site of the Wisconsin Medical Society, "Blind Tom—A 19th Century Marvelous Musician," www.wisconsinmedicalsociety.org/savant/blindtom.cfm.

89 *"On a personal level . . ."* Ibid., "Leslie Lemke: An Inspirational Performance," www.wisconsinmedical-society.org/savant/lemke.cfm.

91 *"In totality . . ."* Interview with Darold A. Treffert, MD.

92 *Although the left-brain/right-brain concept* "Music and Brain Research: Sweeter Music All the Time," *Education Digest,* November 2000, 49–54.

93 *"As is the case . . ."* DeBlois archives.

95 *Dr. Treffert describes the savant memory* Darold A. Treffert, MD, *Extraordinary People: Understanding Savant Syndrome,* 223.

96 *"I've come to believe . . ."* Interview with Darold A. Treffert, MD.

97 *"This level of memory . . ."* Ibid.

98 *"Langdon practiced . . ."* Darold A. Treffert, MD, *Extraordinary People: Understanding Savant Syndrome,* 77.

99 *"Autism, especially in its . . ."* Interview with Darold A. Treffert, MD.

100 *"The unique nature . . ."* Ibid.

101 *"It isn't exploitation . . ."* Ibid.

103 *"It's interesting . . ."* Ibid.

105 *"I still marvel at it . . ."* Ibid.

Chapter Four

107 *"It is highly likely . . ."* Leon K. Miller, *Musical Savants: Exceptional Skill in the Mentally Retarded* (Hillsdale, NJ: Lawrence Erlbaum, 1989), 162.

123 *"Tony walks maintaining . . ."* DeBlois archives.

124 *"Tony prefers playing . . ."* Ibid.

133 *"It is 3:30 in the morning . . ."* "Foster parenting means work . . . and satisfaction," Black Hills Special Services Cooperative newsletter.

134 *When Tony came to Bieber's studio*   Interview with Marianne Bieber.

137 *"His hearing is . . . "*   "Special Guidance for Gifted Pianist," *Daily Call* (Lead, SD), April 23, 1983, 1.

Chapter Five

139 *"Your sound is like . . . "*   Ben Sidran, *Talking Jazz: An Illustrated Oral History* (San Francisco: Pomegranate Artbooks, 1992), 5.

140 *"After playing together . . ."*   Interview with Bo Winiker.

151 *A self-described*   Interview with Marc Cabot.

152 *"Sometimes, when blind students . . ."*   Interview with Adele Trytko.

154 *"When I first met Tony . . ."*   Interview with Storm Barkus.

159 *"I had never taught . . . "*   Interview with Paul Barringer.

165 *"Tony walked to the piano . . ."*   DeBlois archives.

169 *"It is my opinion . . ."*   Ibid.

170 *"Tony is already well equipped . . ."*   Ibid.

172 *". . . landmark step . . ."*   "Living in a World of Music," *Boston Globe*, May 13, 1990, 25.

172 *"What is important . . ."*   Ibid.

177 *"When the set was over . . ."*   Interview with Bill Winiker.

178 *"It was the most incredible thing . . ."*   Interview with Bo Winiker.

181 *"A flower blossoming . . ."*   Ibid.

181 *"If anything . . ."*   Interview with Bo Winiker.

Chapter Six

183 *"In jazz, you are . . ."* Ben Sidron, *Talking Jazz: An Illustrated Oral History* (San Francisco: Pomegranate Artbooks, 1992), 144.

185 *As he played* John LaPorta, *Playing It By Ear* (Redwood, NY: North Country Distributors, 2001), 210.

186 *"LaPorta was ecstatic . . ."* Interview with Gregory Badolato.

187 *"You have to realize . . ."* Ibid.

189 *"I think they wanted . . ."* Interview with Suzanna Sifter.

189 *"When I leaned over . . ."* Ibid.

190 *"He would continue . . ."* Ibid.

191 *"I taught him a classical piece . . ."* Ibid.

192 *"When he got up . . ."* Ibid.

197 *"Ear training is taught . . ."* Interview with Gregory Badolato.

197 *"That's actually grasping . . ."* Interview with Rob Rose.

198 *a musician "who's not really hung up . . ."* *Today Show,* August 12, 1991, videotape transcribed by the author.

199 *"It was very evident . . ."* Interview with Rob Rose.

199 *"You have to edit yourself . . ."* Interview with Gregory Badolato.

Chapter Seven

222 *"We have people . . ."* TheBostonChannel.com, "Musician With Savant Syndrome Performs for Mayor," November 11, 2003, www.thebostonchannel.com/ news/ 2629527/detail.html.

225 *"It is the nature . . ."* Vatican Web site, "Message of the Holy Father to the Youth of the World on

the Occasion of the XVII World Youth Day,"
www.vatican.va/ holy_father/john_paul_ii/
messages/ youth/documents/hf_jp-ii_mes_
20010731_xvii-world-youth-day_en.html.

229 *"Your children are not . . ."* Kahlil Gibran, *The Prophet* (Columbia University online edition, www.columbia.edu/~gm84/gibtable.html.)

RESOURCES

Suggested Reading

Aronson, Virginia. *Different Minds, Different Voices.* Boca Raton, FL: Paradux and Gossling, 1996.

Losier, Dave. *Fred's Prayer Machine.* Worcester, MA: Ambassador Books, 2002. (Author's note: This children's story features Tony as a character in a classroom setting.)

Miller, Leon K. *Musical Savants: Musical Skill in the Mentally Retarded.* Hillsdale, NJ: Erlbaum, 1989.

Treffert, Darold A., MD. *Extraordinary People: Understanding Savant Syndrome,* 2nd ed. Lincoln, NE: iUniverse.com, 2000.

Related Web Sites

Tony DeBlois's Official Web Site

www.tonydeblois.com

Dr. Treffert's Savant Syndrome Site for the Wisconsin Medical Society

www.savantsyndrome.com

Autism Society of America

www.autism-society.org

Video Clip of Tony DeBlois at Millennium Stage on July 28, 2000

www.kennedycenter.org/programs/millennium/ artist_detail.cfm?artist_id=VSAARTSVSA

Discography

Some Kind of Genius (2005)

Tony DeBlois, piano, vocals, trumpet on track 3, alto sax on track 14

Bo Winiker, trumpet, flügelhorn, vocals on track 5 with Tony

Tom Petrakis, bass

Bill Winiker, drums

Twin Tune Productions (www.tonydeblois.com)

Track listing:

1. Strike Up the Band

2. Pensativa

3. Muskrat Ramble

4. Tony's Blues

5. Lady Be Good

6. Joy Spring

7. Indian Summer

8. Sunday, Monday or Always

9. Drop Me Off in Harlem

10. Almost Like Being in Love

11. Sentimental Over You

12. Mexican Hip Dance

13. Twin Tune

14. Don't Get Around Much Anymore

Thrice as Nice (2004)

Tony Deblois, piano, vocals, alto sax

Bo Winiker, trumpet and flügelhorn

Tom Patrakis, bass

Bill Winiker, drums

Ed Fiorenza, tenor sax (and piano on track 4)

Twin Tune Productions
(www.tonydeblois.com)

Track listing:

1. Let It Snow
2. Winter Wonderland
3. Sleigh Ride
4. Christmas Time Is Here
5. O Christmas Tree
6. Silent Night
7. Away in a Manger
8. We Three Kings of Orient Are
9. Hark! The Herald Angels Sing
10. Christmas Waltz
11. The Christmas Song
12. Joyful, Joyful, We Adore You
13. Ave Maria
14. What Child Is This
15. When the Holiday Is Over
16. Have Yourself a Merry Little Christmas

Mercer, Mercy Me (2003)

Tony Deblois, piano and vocals

Bo Winiker, trumpet and flügelhorn

Tom Patrakis, bass

Bill Winiker, drums

Twin Tune Productions
(www.tonydeblois.com)

Track listing:

1. Too Marvelous for Words
2. If I Had a Million Dollars
3. Blues in the Night
4. Tangerine
5. Summer Wind

6. Satin Doll
7. Dearly Beloved
8. Skylark
9. Jeepers Creepers
10. Moon River
11. I Thought About You
12. I Remember You
13. Goody, Goody
14. Emily
15. Dream

Beyond Words (2002)

Tony DeBlois, piano
Twin Tune Productions
(www.tonydeblois.com)
Track listing:
1. All the Things You Are
2. I'm Old Fashioned
3. Prelude to a Kiss
4. Tony's Blues
5. My Funny Valentine
6. Twin Tune
7. Body and Soul
8. I Got Rhythm
9. Round Midnight

Four Thousand Years of Music (1999)

Tony DeBlois, piano
Cornerstone Christian Music Worldwide
(www.cdfreedom.com/tonydeblois)
Track listing:
1. Sumerian Hymn to Creation
2. Sumer Is Icumen In

3. The Carman's Whistle

4. Invention in C (J. S. Bach)

5. Jesu, Joy of Man's Desiring (J. S. Bach)

6. For Unto Us a Child Is Born (Handel)

7. Rondo à la Turk (Mozart)

8. "Moonlight" Sonata, mvt. I (Beethoven)

9. Ode to Joy (Beethoven)

10. Ave Maria (Schubert)

11. Raindrop Prelude (Chopin)

12. Traumerei (Schumann)

13. Lullaby (Brahms)

14. Overture from the *Nutcracker Suite* (Tchaikovsky)

15. Russian Dance *(Nutcracker Suite)*

16. Waltz of the Flowers *(Nutcracker Suite)*

17. Pas de Deux *(Nutcracker Suite)*

18. Dance of the Sugar Plum Fairy *(Nutcracker Suite)*

19. Reverie (Debussy)

20. Meditation on the Lord's Prayer (Romeo)

Thank God for Life! (1999)
Tony DeBlois, piano and vocals
Alice Fraleigh, Eric Lindahl, and Lyndé Weston, background vocals
Eric Lindahl, flute
Jim Sharrock, oboe
Jim Lounsbury, violin
Emily Singer, cello
Freddy Rizzo, acoustic/electric guitar
Cornerstone Christian Music Worldwide
(www.cdfreedom.com/tonydeblois)
Track listing:

1. Thank God for Life!

2. Pilgrimage 2000

3. Song of Praise

4. Prayer to Mary

5. Connected

6. Born to Serve God

7. Fatima Family Apostolate Hymn

8. You Care!

9. Peaceful Night

10. Miracles

11. Littlest Babe, Mightiest King

12. Beautiful Angel

13. Sing Joyfully!

14. Meditation on the Lord's Prayer

Contact Information

For correspondence and CD orders:

Janice DeBlois

31 Cochato Park

Randolph, MA 02368-4209

e-mail: JanDeBlois@aol.com

Tony DeBlois's Official Web Site:

www.tonydeblois.com

For CD orders:

www.cdfreedom.com/tonydeblois